aPHR Study Guide 2021-2022

aPHR Exam Prep + 300 Questions for the Associate Professional in Human Resources Certification (Includes 3 Full-Length Tests with Detailed Answer Explanations)

Table of Contents

About the Associate Professional in Human Resources Certification

The aPHR exam is specifically for those who have just entered the workforce or who are planning to begin a career in the field of human resources (HR). Obtaining a certification in the field of human resources is an important step to take when seeking a career in this field. The Human Resources Certification Institute (HRCI) was founded in 1976. It is the only internationally recognized group that certifies people in HR.

Pearson VUE, an international testing agency, administers the Associate Professional in Human Resources exam, also known as the aPHR.

There is a six-step process to becoming certified as an Associate Professional in Human Resources:

1. Ensure that you meet the requirements to be eligible to take the aPHR exam.
2. Apply to take the aPHR exam through the HRCI.
3. Find a Pearson VUE Testing Center near you and schedule your appointment to take either an in-person or online exam.
4. Prepare for the exam you are about to take, using books like this study guide.
5. Take your aPHR exam.
6. Once the exam is complete, you will receive an email from Pearson VUE that will inform you that your scores are ready to be viewed on the Pearson VUE website. If you pass the exam, you will then receive your proof of certification. Pearson VUE and the HRCI offer a digital badge or a paper certificate at the expense of the examinee.

The information that is contained in the aPHR exam, for the most part, requires that you have work experience–based knowledge and understanding. You can find more information about the requirements you need to meet in order to qualify to apply to take the aPHR exam by visiting https://www.hrci.org/our-programs/our-certifications/aphr.

The HRCI webpage has a section that outlines its code of ethics for HR personnel, as well as a detailed explanation of all certifications offered. Further information can be found at the HRCI's website at http://www.hrci.org.

Arranging to Take Your aPHR Exam

The one requirement to qualify to take the aPHR is a high school diploma or a general education development certificate (GED) or the equivalent to a high school diploma based on where the individual is located globally.

The application for the aPHR exam must be filled out online.

Applying to Take Your aPHR Exam through HRCI

To submit an application, visit the HRCI website at http://www.hrci.org. Click on the Apply Now icon at the top of the webpage. This icon will take you to the HRCI log-in page. Once on the log-in page, click the Create New Account option. The website will walk you through each of the steps that need to be completed in order to create an account for the HRCI. Once the account has been set up, you will be returned to the original log-in page.

- Please Note: Any qualified individual who lives in the United States or Canada will also have the option to use Pearson VUE's OnVUE online proctoring program as an alternative to the Pearson VUE in-person examination. However, there are some requirements and restrictions that will be explained later in this study guide for those wishing to pursue this option.

Once you have created your initial HRCI account, log in. The username will be the email you listed, followed by the password you created when you set up your account. It is essential to save your log-in information for your personal records.

Once logged in, select the My Application tab and choose the appropriate exam. Understand that HRCI and Pearson VUE will list more than just the aPHR exam as a testing option, so it is essential to know which exam you are choosing and to select the correct one when signing up for the exam.

For the purposes of this study guide, choose the aPHR exam. The HRCI site will provide you with options to choose the items you want to be included in your application packet. This will consist of the actual aPHR exam, and then you will be offered optional HRCI-specific prep materials for an additional fee.

Once you have made your selections, confirm your choices, verify that the information you provided is correct and agree to the HRCI handbook policies and procedures. Once that has been completed, pay the application fee, and then you will be able to submit your application.

- There is a fee of $100 that you will be required to pay at the time you submit your application. In addition to the application fee, you will also have the option to purchase second chance insurance (SCI) for an additional cost. SCI is not required and is *only* offered at the time the application is being submitted.

Once your exam fee is paid, and the application is submitted, the HRCI will review your application. You will then receive an email from the HRCI. The email will inform you of your application status. You will either be told that your application has been approved, that the HRCI needs you to submit further information before it can proceed with approving your application, that your application has been chosen for an audit at random or that your application has been declined. If your application is rejected, the email will include information on the steps that you can take next and how you can reapply to take the exam.

From the time that your application is approved, you will have up to four months or 120 days to make an appointment with Pearson VUE and take your aPHR exam. This is known as the exam eligibility period.

If, for any reason, you have not made an appointment or have failed to take your exam by the time the 120 days expire, you will be required to reapply to take your chosen exam through the HRCI.

More About Second Chance Insurance for the aPHR exam

SCI insurance costs an additional $250 and is nonrefundable for those who purchase it. The benefit of buying SCI is that it allows applicants to retake the exact same exam that they took on their first attempt.

It is essential to understand that the fee for SCI is not refundable regardless of whether or not you use it. If you do not need to retake the exam, you will not be refunded the $250 fee.

It is also of great importance to know that if you do not purchase SCI and you are unable to pass the aPHR exam on your first attempt, you will be given an alternative version to the aPHR exam to the test that you attempted on the first try.

Fees Associated with Signing Up for and Taking the Associate Professional in Human Resources Exam

The following are the fees associated with taking the aPHR exam:

- Application Fee $100.00
- Exam Fee $300.00
- Second Chance Insurance $250.00
- Exam Retake Fee $100.00
- Rescheduling/Cancelation Fee $150.00

Rescheduling or Canceling Your Pearson VUE or Pearson OnVUE Exam

The rescheduling and cancelation fee for the aPHR exam will apply every single time an in-person exam is rescheduled or canceled if that exam is scheduled at a Pearson VUE testing center.

In the event that your exam is scheduled through the Pearson OnVUE online proctored testing system, you will have up until the day of the scheduled exam to reschedule or cancel. All Pearson OnVUE exams can be rescheduled or canceled without the penalty of a fee. Additionally, once you have rescheduled your exam, you will receive an email from Pearson OnVUE confirming the new appointment.

Payments and Fees for the HRCI

The HRCI allows applicants to pay their application fees and other associated testing material and certification fees using the following methods:

- Debit and Credit Card:
  - Visa
  - Mastercard
  - American Express
- Money Order
- Cashier's Check
- Business Check

Cash is not accepted by the HRCI or Pearson VUE as a payment method in the United States. Debit cards, credit cards, money orders and cashier's checks are the most widely accepted forms of payment for examinees internationally. However, countries outside of the United States may allow cash and other forms of payment, so it is essential that individuals confirm with their local testing facilities what payment methods are available to them. Company, organization and nonprofit checks are also accepted under specific guidelines.

For further information on the payment options available or more specific payment details for your location, contact the HRCI, Pearson VUE or a testing site close to you.

Incomplete payments for either HRCI or Pearson VUE will result in your application being declined, and you will be required to restart the application and registration process from the beginning.

All payments must be made in the form of United States dollars. Checks of any kind can only be from a United States bank.

Those who use a cashier's check or money order can expect their applications or exam appointments to be marked as pending until payment is received and processed. When not paying with a debit or credit card, the HRCI requires you to complete your digital forms online, print your application summary and then mail a copy of the application summary along with the type of payment you have chosen. Your application will not be reviewed for approval by the HRCI until after it has received your payment, and the payment has cleared.

Payments and Fees for Pearson VUE Testing Facilities

Pearson VUE accepts the following forms of payment in the United States, Canada and select countries internationally:

- Debit or Credit Card:
  - VISA
  - Mastercard
  - American Express
  - JCB

For individuals in most countries, all payments for Pearson VUE testing are required to be made before the day of testing. Examinees will not be allowed to make payments at the testing facility at any time, including the day of testing.

Credit card payments are not accepted in Afghanistan, Bangladesh, Benin, Cameroon, Gambia, Ghana, Lebanon, Nigeria, Pakistan, Senegal, Tanzania, Tango and Uganda. Because of this, those who test in these countries will be allowed to make their payments in person at the testing facility on testing day.

More specifically, if you are in a country in which Pearson VUE does not allow you to pay online via a debit or credit card, you will need to contact your local testing facility to find out the exact forms of payment that they accept before your exam. Internationally, locations and accepted payment forms will vary.

Pearson VUE accepts most payments online. Those who use a cashier's check or money order can expect their applications or exam appointments to be marked as pending until payment is received and processed.

HRCI and Pearson VUE Payment Vouchers: How to Apply for Them and More

Both the HRCI and Pearson VUE have payment vouchers that are specific to their respective company. Vouchers from the HRCI and from Pearson VUE are not interchangeable between the two companies. However, each company does have a program for cashing in payment vouchers.

Vouchers from the HRCI and Pearson VUE are valid for twelve months or 365 days from the date on which they are issued. Vouchers are not exchangeable or interchangeable. In the event that your voucher expires or you use your voucher to pay for an exam but fail to take that exam within 120 days, you will then be required to pay new fees or purchase new vouchers.

Anyone interested in obtaining a Pearson VUE voucher should visit http://www.pearsonvue.com/vouchers/pricelist/symantec.asp

Vouchers for the HRCI can be obtained by emailing vouchers@hrci.org. You can view and print additional information by going to https://www.hrci.org/docs/default-source/toolkits/voucher-provider-instruction.pdf?sfvrsn=96da4861_2.

Scheduling and Testing - At the Center

Once your application has been approved by the HRCI, you may then schedule your appointment with Pearson VUE. It is recommended that individuals schedule exam appointments as soon as possible.

Once on the Pearson VUE website, http://www.pearsonvue.com/hrci/, you will create a log-in and schedule your exam. Before scheduling your exam, make sure that you:

- Ensure that the name you use on your application matches the name on the identification which you will be providing at the time of your examination.
- Have the nine-digit eligibility number that the HRCI will issue you at the time of your application. This will most often be included in an email or letter sent to the applicant.
- Have a good contact number that you can be reached at during daytime and business hours.
- Know the type of exam that you need to take. For the purposes of this study guide, that will be the aPHR exam.
- Know the location of the testing site that is most convenient for you. Consider having more than one location in mind in case your first choice is not available.
- Know the date and time preference that you have for taking your exam.
- Have a valid email address where you can be reached.

NOTE TO EXAM TAKERS: It is essential to understand that due to the current pandemic, in-person appointments may be canceled or rescheduled through Pearson VUE.

In the event that this occurs, the application fee that was paid when the exam was scheduled initially will be applied to the new appointment. There will not be any new appointment or application fees required for any cancelations or changes that are made by Pearson VUE in the interest of public health and safety.

Contact your local convenient testing center to verify that they are taking appointments and/or to confirm any particular policies. Examinees may also find a restriction or limitation on the number of testing spaces available, the number of examinees that will be accepted for testing per day or the number of testing sessions that may occur on a daily basis.

Be aware that additional time for check-ins may be necessary, and longer times between tests may be necessary to allow for the cleaning of common areas and testing sites.

Pearson VUE is also offering an online live proctoring examination program for some exams in select countries. More information on that testing option is discussed below.

Exam Day

Ensure that you get plenty of rest the night before the exam. Arrive fifteen to thirty minutes prior to the start of your exam to allow yourself ample time to check in.

Ensure that you have a valid driver's license or other approved form of identification. Ensure that the name on your identification is exactly the same as the one you used when you completed your application. If the names do not match, you may not be allowed to take your exam. In addition to valid identification, be sure to bring your appointment letter, and anything else that you have been told is required. Be sure not to bring any nonessential items with you.

Once the examinees for that time slot have all been checked in, you will be taken into the testing room and assigned a seat. The exam instructor will go over the rules for the exam. Once the exam begins, you will not be permitted to get up or leave the testing room until you have finished the exam.

Scheduling and Testing - Online Proctor Exams

Pearson VUE offers residents of the United States and Canada examinations through an online live proctoring program known as Pearson OnVUE. The program allows you to register for your exam online. Then, at the time of the exam, it enables you to take your proctored exam online rather than in-person at one of the Pearson VUE testing facilities.

In order to take your exam through the Pearson OnVUE program, you must:

- Do a computer system check on the computer that you intend to use for the exam to ensure that your computer capabilities meet the exam requirements.
- Do an internet speed test to ensure that your internet speed is adequate for taking the examination. (In the event that the internet speed is not sufficient, you can have your internet speed adjusted at your own expense, and then retest your internet's speed capabilities.)
- Have a working webcam available for live monitoring and recording during the official proctored exam.

All of the examinees who choose the Pearson OnVUE online proctoring exam are required to give their express consent in order to be live online with the testing proctor during the exam. The proctored exam is recorded on a webcam and live monitored from the time you begin the exam until its conclusion.

The rules, policies and procedures for the Pearson OnVUE exam are much the same as those for anyone taking the exam in person, with few exceptions. Examinees who choose to take the exam online will be permitted to reschedule their OnVUE exam appointments up to the date and time that their exam is scheduled. Cancelation of OnVUE appointments are treated much the same and can be canceled up until the day of the exam and any time prior to its scheduled time. Online exam appointments may be rescheduled or canceled without penalty to the examinee.

The HRCI will have examinees' unofficial test results within one hour of the completion of the OnVUE online proctored exam. The official results from

Pearson VUE will be between 24 and 48 hours after the official exam has been completed.

Pearson Vue will send an email to each individual when official scores are ready for viewing. To be clear, the HRCI website will simply offer individuals notification of passing or failing the test. To obtain the actual numerical score for the exam, individuals will need to log in to their personal Pearson VUE account. Once logged in, individuals will be able to view their full test scores.

The HRCI website provides further details on policies, rules and procedures. It also offers the option to contact the organization for further information not answered in the questions and answers tab.

OnVUE Special Accommodations Notice

Pearson VUE offers special testing accommodations for those who qualify. However, those accommodations are only currently offered for in-person exams. The online proctoring system does not currently have the capabilities to allow for accommodations.

Rules for OnVUE Online Proctored Exams

Most of the rules for Pearson VUE exams are the same as the Pearson OnVUE online proctored exam. However, there are a few rules that are specific to the Pearson OnVUE live proctored exams.

1. Examinees are required to have a clean testing area where they can take their exam.

2. The testing space where the exam will be taken must be distraction-free and private.

3. Examinees are required to stay in full view of their webcam during each testing session, in sight of the proctor and must stay seated while testing is in progress.

4. Outside of any scheduled breaks provided by the testing proctor, examinees will not be allowed to take breaks.

Any examinee who gets up or leaves for an unscheduled or unapproved reason during any portion of the exam will find the exam is immediately ended, and any part of the exam that has been completed will be void.

Exam Day for OnVUE

On the day of the exam, you will be given instructions on how to check in online for the proctored exam. As part of the check-in process, you will be connected with a Pearson VUE greeter.

The greeter will send you a URL link that requires you to upload a copy of your photo identification, a selfie at the time of check-in and pictures of the space that you plan to be testing in.

In order to continue with the exam, the Pearson VUE greeter will approve the photos that you have uploaded in order to:

1. Confirm that the individual that is signed up for the exam is also the individual that is checking in and taking the online proctored exam.

2. Ensure that the examination space meets the requirements to take the exam.

The greeter will also require individuals to turn on their webcam and show their testing space live to ensure that the testing space meets all of Pearson VUE requirements for the OnVUE live proctoring exam online.

Once the check-in process has been completed and you, your computer and your testing space have all been approved, you will then be put in touch with the proctor who will be overseeing your exam.

What if I Lose Internet or My Computer Glitches While Live During My Online Proctored OnVUE Exam?

In the event that you have a technical issue during the live online exam, the proctor will make every effort to reestablish the connection and allow you to continue the exam.

However, in the event that you and the proctor are not able to reestablish a connection, the proctor will be responsible for officially ending the session for your OnVUE exam. You will then be required to reschedule your exam appointment.

Results and Receiving Your Credentials

The comprehensive exam scores can be viewed online within 48 hours, by logging into your personal HRCI-Pearson Vue account.

A passing score for the aPHR exam is 500/700 or greater. If your score falls below the minimum passing score, you will be required to retake the exam. If your score is higher than 500/700, you will be considered to have passed your exam and will be able to collect your certification.

The HRCI uses a digital badge, which is a new technique for certification. The digital badges are certified and can be used on almost any electronic platform. Additionally, all applicants will be given the option to receive a paper copy of their certification as well. While the digital badges are provided to examinees upon passing their exam, a paper copy of the certification can be provided at an additional cost. Please visit the Human Resources Certification Institute website at www.hrci.org to get the most current fee for a hard copy of your HRCI credentials.

Topics to Review

The aPHR exam has six key areas. The fields of study that you will need to familiarize yourself with include:

1. Human Resources Operations – 38% of the exam
2. Recruitment and Selection – 15% of the exam
3. Compensation and Benefits – 14% of the exam
4. Human Resources Development and Retention – 12% of the exam
5. Employee Relations – 16% of the exam
6. Health, Safety and Security – 5% of the exam

Human Resources Professionals

Human resources professionals will develop a wealth of knowledge as they grow in their careers. This knowledge will include employment, placement, personnel planning, training and development, compensation and benefits, health, safety, security, employee relations, labor relations and management practices.

Being an HR professional is about honing your role, which will help you to ensure that things run in a smooth, efficient manner.

Tips for Studying

Consider the following when preparing for the exam:

- What are your strengths and weaknesses?
- Ensure that you have familiarized yourself with the HRCI's testing guidelines and understand what information you need to focus on when studying.
- Decide on the study methods that work best for you. These could include:
    - Making flash cards out of the materials you find in this study guide in order to better review the information.
    - Taking the practice tests in this book to understand areas where you excel and what you may yet need to work on.

    - Reviewing the materials more than once or making notes on the information you feel needs extra review.
- Set up a timetable to allow yourself to sufficiently study before you take the official exam.
    - Start studying a sufficient amount of time before you schedule your exam.
    - Ensure that you dedicate more time to reviewing areas that you do not know as well.
    - Consider alternative study methods:
        - Study groups
        - Study partners
        - Studying alone
        - Studying online with others
        - Prep courses

Key Points in Human Resources to Review

The following is a list of the critical topics of study that you will need to know when preparing to take your aPHR exam. Following this list, you will find further explanations on many of these topics. The topics below are the information you should know about any organization that you are performing HR duties for, the laws that apply to them and to you as an HR professional and the laws that apply to employees and employee rights. Note that for the purposes of this book, the terms *organization, business* and *company* are used interchangeably.

- A business' mission, plans and goals to meet that mission.
- The laws and regulations that apply to an organization and how these are implemented and carried out.
- The strategies for meeting an organization's goals and how it plans to implement and achieve those goals.
- The role management will play in an organization, the levels that the organization will have and how it plans to organize the members of management.

- How a corporation will be governed, the procedures and compliance that will be put in place for its operations and the way in which it will implement its governance.
- The cost-benefit analysis that will be conducted throughout the life of the business, as well as its net worth and earnings data.
- Advertising, branding and corporate responsibility.
- Laws and regulations that apply to a business.
- Reviewing and assessing staff needs and the cost of staff.
- Creating and utilizing recruitment strategies, recruiting qualified employees, encouraging employee referrals and attracting appropriate candidates.
- Alternative staffing choices, such as dual-training, job sharing, outsourcing such as temporary employment agencies and staggered retirement of employees.
- Determining what the needs of an organization will be in the future.

- Interviewing styles:
    - One-on-one interviews, also known as individual interviews.
    - Panel interviews, where an employment candidate goes before three or more members of a business in order to interview. For example, the employment candidate may be interviewed by a panel made up of a member of HR, the person who will be the individual's direct supervisor and the head of the entire department.
    - Multi-round interviews. In these kinds of interviews, candidates may go in for an interview and meet with an entry-level HR employee. The person doing the initial interviews will arrange to have the candidates who seem to meet all of the qualifications return to meet with a more experienced member of HR. This process often involves eliminating candidates at each round of interviews until the most qualified and best-fitting candidates are left to choose from.

- Compensation, Benefits and Retirement Packages:
    - Health-Care Insurance
    - Dental Insurance
    - Vision Insurance
    - Life Insurance
    - Unemployment Compensation
    - Workers' Compensation
    - Vacation Pay
    - Holiday Pay
    - Paid Time Off (PTO) Accrual
    - 401K Plan or Pension Plan
    - Stock Options
    - Maternity Leave – Paid
    - Paternity Leave – Paid
    - Profit-Sharing
    - Bonuses

- Termination:
    - Voluntary termination occurs when an employee resigns from a position either in writing or verbally. Voluntary termination can also encompass an employee's intent to retire, or when an employee is a "no call, no show" and abandons a position.
    - Involuntary termination occurs when an employee is fired or otherwise forced out of a job. The type of business, or where in the world the employment occurs, will also determine if the employer needs any reason at all in order to terminate an employee.
    - Downsizing occurs when a business lowers the number of employees in order to streamline or cut costs.

    - Restructuring occurs when an organization cuts the number of employees in order to make things run more efficiently and generate a more significant profit.

- The workforce within a company and its demographics
- Policies, practices and procedures as they pertain to employment
- Employment negotiations
- Creating, testing, implementing and improving training and development techniques
- Techniques and methods used for program delivery, instruction, teaching and facilitation
- Performance reviews, merit raises or bonuses, career development and promotions
- Career advancements and career ladder planning and goal setting
- Vetting of training and career development programs to ascertain their effectiveness, and reevaluating techniques that appear to be failing or having a less than desirable effect
- Understanding the budgeting for a business, organization or department; evaluating budgets in regard to benefits and compensation
- Methods of evaluating jobs and determining pay scales
- External labor markets and the economy
- Equity programs and stock options
- Legal responsibilities relating to benefits and compensation to employees
- Employment unions and non-unions
- Positive employee relations and the techniques used to facilitate them
- Staff meetings, work teams and other committees and groups within the workplace
- Behavior, behavioral issues, respect and disrespect in the workplace

- Compensation programs and procedures for employees who are injured at work and the programs in place to mitigate workplace injuries and illnesses
- Risk Management:
    - Safety for the employees and within the workplace
    - Health of employees and ensuring that the business is not causing any undue harm to its staff
    - Risk prevention
    - Investigative options when health-related illnesses or injuries occur in the workplace
- Processes and procedures for returning to work after illness or injury
- Workplace violence and hostile environments
- Emergency and disaster situation planning, protocol and procedures
- Internal business security, biometrics, monitoring software and other security software
- Choosing vendors, negotiating contracts and otherwise working with outside vendors and contractors
- Project management
- Diversity in the workplace
- Professional and ethical standards.
- Budgets, accounting and finance as relates to HR and business.

Next, you will find additional study materials to help prepare you for the aPHR. Most of this information has been broken down by exam topic to better outline the skills and knowledge you will need to know for each of the criteria that will appear on the exam.

Human Resources Operations

The size of a business will significantly determine its HR needs and the size of the HR department that will be required. Limited liability partnerships, limited liability companies and small businesses often use an outside source to manage their HR needs because they are too small to need a full-scale HR department. The larger the company or organization, the more its HR needs are likely to expand, and the more likely the company is to be better served by an HR department.

HR personnel wear many hats. The primary operations for an HR department often include administrative services, recruiting new employees, analyzing job needs within a business and taking part in and facilitating employee/employer relationships.

The purpose of an HR department is ultimately to support an organization's owners, managers and staff in conducting their daily business, meeting their immediate needs and achieving the organization's long-term goals.

Human resources acts on an administrative level by providing payroll services and management, entering initial new employee information and maintaining a business' employee information through a database that can be periodically updated, ensuring that an organization is checking in with its employees and ensuring their satisfaction with their positions and maintaining various personnel tasks.

Another important task that the HR department undertakes is analyzing jobs within a business. Job analysis is a crucial task for any business because it is about outlining the duties and responsibilities within an organization, the exact details required to get those jobs completed, the number of people needed to effectively complete these jobs and the skills necessary for an individual to competently complete the work.

Human resources professionals are responsible for creating a database that will house the jobs throughout the organization. This database includes a detailed explanation of what the job entails, a system for tracking whether the positions are filled or vacant and a detailed outline of what skills a potential candidate should have in order to fill a vacancy in any of the positions.

Parts of HR operations include recruitment, selection, compensation, benefits, training, development, employee retention, employee relations and safety and risk management. These will be discussed in more detail in the sections below.

The Three Key Components of Human Resources Management and Operations

The three critical components of HR management and operations include knowledge, skills and abilities.

Human resources knowledge includes:

- Knowing the basic processes and procedures as they pertain to the role of HR in an organization
- Clerical abilities, including but not limited to the knowledge of the staff as it pertains to word processing, file management, record-keeping, office procedures and in-field terminology
- Administrative and management skills. This includes business, management, strategic planning, allocating resources, leadership techniques and the methods used within production
- Ability to serve people and customers alike. This is done by knowing business practices and adhering to their core principles, meeting personnel and customer service needs, setting and meeting service standards and meeting customer satisfaction standards.

Next, meeting the needed skills of HR personnel means:

- Knowing how to actively listen by paying attention to detail
- Being able to understand the points being made
- Asking follow-up questions for needed clarification
- Understanding when to listen and when to speak up.

Finally, to effectively work in HR operations and management, personnel need to have the ability to understand and use verbal communication and written communication. These attributes are all key to an individual succeeding in the HR world.

Human Resources Operations and How it Applies to Workplace Signage

A role that falls under HR operations is workplace signage. Workplace signs are federally required to be posted in every business so long as an organization has employees. Such signage must be placed in clear view and in a location that employees are known to frequent. These locations can include employee break rooms or locker rooms.

This federal signage includes:

- Family and Medical Leave Act poster –must be posted in all businesses with fifty employees or more.

- Occupational Safety and Health Act (OSHA) poster – must be posted in all businesses with any employees. In addition to this federally mandated poster, some states have their own state-mandated signs as well.

- Fair Labor Standards Act poster – must be posted in all businesses with any employees. The U.S. Department of Labor distributes this poster.

- Notice to Workers with Disabilities Act (also known as Special Minimum Wage) – required at a minimum for all employers who have employees with disabilities. However, many employers post the sign as standard practice, regardless.

- Employee Polygraph Protection Act poster – must be posted in all businesses with employees.

- Minimum Wage poster – must be posted in all businesses with employees.

Recruitment & Selection

Starting up and continuing to run a business successfully is all about the people who work for that organization and the jobs they do within it. It is vital to attract and hire the right people to your team to have a successful business. So, HR professionals have a lot on their shoulders when it comes to advertising jobs, sifting through applications, interviewing candidates and eventually choosing who they will hire.

Job Analysis and Creating a Job Database Within an Organization

Job analysis starts with knowing what jobs there are in a given organization. It includes working with upper management and department heads to determine the exact details of each position within a business. These details are compiled into a portfolio. This portfolio outlines all of the jobs for the entire organization, all of the tasks and requirements that need to be filled under the umbrella of each job and a list of the skills any potential candidates will need in order to fill the position adequately.

Advertising for Employment

The HR department uses the job analysis information to advertise positions that need to be filled. Advertising is geared towards the target candidates that a business needs. For start-up businesses, a wider net is cast to fill a broader range of positions.

The Application Process

If an application process is too complicated or takes too long, then it is less likely that qualified candidates will take the time to complete the process. A simple, seamless and straightforward method is key. Companies that have applications that can be accessed not only on paper but also online and on mobile devices have the most significant record of success.

Reviewing Applications, Tracking Candidate Applications through the Reviewing Process and Choosing the Right Candidates to Interview

Human resources personnel comb through every application that a company receives. Candidates that meet the minimum requirements for a given position are separated for consideration. HR will choose the most qualified individuals for interviews.

Many organizations have multilevel interviewing processes. These start with entry-level personnel meetings with applicants. The candidates who pass the first round of interviews often meet with team leaders or department heads next. The candidates who are chosen to continue after that point usually meet with upper management or the hiring team of the HR department.

Hiring Qualified Candidates

Once the HR department has narrowed down the candidates' list for a given job, HR will offer the chosen candidate a position. The candidate will then work with the hiring agent to negotiate an acceptable contract. A hiring contract will usually outline, in detail, the requirements of the job. It will further describe the salary being offered and any additional benefits or compensation that the organization is offering.

If a position requires the individual to be hired with the express intent to relocate, work abroad or travel for work, the hiring contract will often make special concessions for that. For example, an organization may offer to pay for moving expenses. Those that will be working abroad or internationally may be provided travel expenses, lodging allowances and other financial support for living in another country. Individuals who are being employed to work in dangerous areas or in risky professions are often offered an additional sum as a means of hazard pay.

More specific detail on benefits and compensation will be discussed later in this study guide.

Orientation and Training

Once new employees are hired, the HR department is most often responsible for new employee orientation, arranging for employees to be professionally trained for the position and acclimating employees with their positions. Some of this acclimation process can include doing employee surveys, touching base with supervising staff to check on new or transferred employees' progress and helping to address any issues that may occur during the initial probationary hiring period.

As part of the orientation process, new employees are provided with a handbook or manual that explains an organization's policies and procedures. It is generally the responsibility of HR to ensure that a signed agreement is returned, stating that the employee has received this material, read it and agrees to abide by the contents of the handbook or manual. Handbooks and employee manuals are legally binding documents, and an employee's signature binds him or her, as well as the business, to the information held within the documents.

Compensation & Benefits within an Organization

Compensation and benefits play a huge role in the type of candidates that a business is able to attract for employment. The number one thing that most people think of in regard to compensation is salary. However, there is so much more to compensation and benefits than salary alone.

Compensation and benefits can vary for a wide array of reasons. Some of the things that one might expect to see as part of a benefits or compensation package can include:

- Bonuses
- Health-Care Benefits
  - Health
  - Dental
  - Vision
  - Short-Term/Long-Term Disability
  - Life Insurance
- Maternity Leave
- Merit Pay
- Overtime Pay
- Paternity Leave
- Profit-Sharing
- PTO Accrual
- Relocation Bonuses
- Retirement or Pension Plans

- Salary
- Sick Leave
- Stock Options
- Sign-On Bonuses

The Importance of Training, Development & Retention to an Organization's Success

Training and development is a pivotal role of the HR department. It ensures that new employees are well versed in how to do their jobs. It also helps to update existing employees on new practices and assists them in advancing up their career ladders.

Employee training usually refers to a new employee's skills and knowledge. Employee development, on the other hand, refers to opportunities for continued education, most often for existing employees.

Training and development are extremely important to the overall retention of employees. In return, retention is important to the success of a business as a whole.

In the ideal work structure, the training and development that a business offers is most often returned by employees through retention and advancements. The key to all of these things is a cohesive system that allows employees to:

- Enjoy their work environment
- Receive adequate benefits and compensation for the job that they are doing
- Have proper initial job training
- Have adequate continued education and development
- Have a positive and healthy professional relationship with their employer.

As an HR professional, it is important to also note the legal and ethical requirements for the training and development of all staff. Depending on the career field and job specifications, some jobs are required to have specific local, state or federally mandated training. For example, teachers are required to complete a specific number of continuing education hours each year to ensure they meet state educational standards.

Employee Relations – Strong Relationships Build Strong Businesses

Employee relations is a key part of HR. Employee relations facilitate the relationship between employees, supervisors, management and business owners, the goal being to maintain and improve relationships with employees. Ensuring that employees feel heard and can communicate with those in a position of authority results in a healthy work environment.

Times will always arise when coworkers, supervisors and managers disagree. So, problem-solving is an important part of HR.

The better maintained a business' employee relations are, and the better the overall communication, the less likely there is to be internal conflict. Morale within the business will also be better, and the business will be more successful as a result.

Risk Management – The Health, Safety and Security of an Organization and its Employees

The key to managing the health, safety, and security of a business is protecting the employees and the owners.

To that end, there are not only standards that companies set for themselves, but also local, state and federal laws that apply. Further along in the study guide, you will find details about the different laws and regulations that HR personnel need to know, but it is important to understand laws such as:

- Workplace Health and Safety
- Workplace Privacy and Confidentiality
- Occupational Safety and Health Act
- Americans with Disabilities Act & Americans with Disabilities Act Amendments Act
- HIPAA

These are just some of the few most important and well-known laws that apply in the field of employment.

Risk management is a fairly straightforward term. It's about managing risks to the organization, employees, employer and consumers.

In addition to local, state and federal laws, risk management includes employee safety such as injury or illness prevention, workers' compensation and workplace safety.

Ensuring that employees are not physically, verbally or emotionally harmed while at work is part of ensuring their safety. When that is not an option, organizations should have policies and procedures in place to help resolve differences, remove threats and restore a safe working environment. It is important for businesses to have crisis management plans in place for the safety of all staff and the business as a whole.

Some organizations offer outside resources that pertain to their employees' personal lives, which can affect the health and safety of their work lives. Some examples include:

- Employers in crisis counseling centers maintain a psychologist on staff. The employees at that crisis center are required to sit down once a month with the psychologist to ensure that they are handling the stress associated with their job and are not becoming overwhelmed or depressed. This allows for an intervention if an employee is not handling the suffering of others well. The psychologist can provide tools to help such an employee better handle the stresses of the job or help that employee find a position that is a better fit for his or her mental and emotional health.

- An employer who offers alcohol and drug treatment programs to staff members. The employer pays for the entire program at no cost to the employees so long as they complete the treatment program.

- A nursing home keeps an employee day care on site. Employees can visit their children on breaks and at lunch. Elderly residents who would like to be visited are allowed to sign up for visitation with kids from the facility's staff day-care center. The program improves the quality of life for lonely residents and also staff, who know their children are being well cared for and can see them during the day.

These are just a few examples of ways that employers can improve their work environments. These practices improve the health, safety and welfare of employees. It is proven that healthy, happy employees work harder, invest more of their time in their jobs and are more likely to stay with their current employer rather than seeking employment elsewhere.

Laws That Human Resources Personnel Should Be Familiar With

A wide array of laws apply to businesses and their operations. While laws change, and it may not be possible to know every single law on the books, there are some laws that are fairly constant and should be familiar to any member of HR.

- Americans with Disabilities Act (ADA)
- Age Discrimination in Employment Act (ADEA)
- Civil Rights Act of 1964 – Title VII
- Clayton Act
- Consolidated Omnibus Budget Reconciliation Act (COBRA)
- Consumer Credit Protection Act (CCPA)
- Dodd-Frank Wall Street Reform and Consumer Protection Act – (Dodd-Frank Act)
- Employee Retirement Income Security Act (ERISA)
- Employment Polygraph Protection Act (EPPA)
- Equal Pay Act (EPA)
- Family and Medical Leave Act (FMLA)
- Fair Credit Reporting Act (FCRA)
- Fair Labor Standards Act (FLSA)
- Federal Employment Compensation Act (FECA)

- Federal Insurance Contributions Act (FICA)
- Federal Unemployment Tax Act (FUTA)
- Genetic Information Nondiscrimination Act (GINA)
- Health Insurance Portability and Accountability Act (HIPAA)
- Immigration and Nationality Act
- Labor-Management Reporting and Disclosure Act (LMRDA)
- Longshore and Harbor Workers' Compensation Act
- National Labor Relations Act (NLRA)
- Norris-La Guardia Act
- Ohio Pregnancy Discrimination Act
- Occupational Safety and Health Act (OSHA)
- Patent Act
- Patient Protection and Affordable Care Act (PPACA – a.k.a. Obamacare)
- Payne vs. the Western & Atlantic Railroad Company
- Portal-to-Portal Act
- Pregnancy Discrimination Act
- Public Contracts Act (PCA)
- Railway Labor Act
- Service Contract Act
- Sherman Antitrust Act
- Social Security Act
- Uniformed Services Employment and Reemployment Rights Act (USERRA)
- Worker Adjustment and Retraining Notification Act (WARN)

Explanation of these Laws and How They Apply to an Organization

I. The **Americans with Disabilities Act** (ADA) applies to local and state government organizations, federal organizations, private employers and all employment and labor agencies or unions. It prevents employers from discriminating against individuals with disabilities as their disability pertains to the application process, interviewing process, hiring process or firing process.

Additionally, an individual's disability may not be considered of any consequence when a person is being considered for promotion, training for a position, furthering current job training or considering employment benefits or compensation.

In summary, the ADA prohibits employers with fifteen or more employees from discriminating against individuals who are otherwise qualified based on their disability. Additionally, it requires an employer to make accommodations for a disabled employee, so long as the accommodations are considered to be reasonable, and those accommodations do not cause excessive harm to the business or employer.

- The **Americans with Disabilities Act Amendments Act,** which was enacted in 2008, and went into effect in 2009, made changes to the original ADA. The amendments covered more disabilities under the Americans with Disabilities Act protections and lowered the threshold for what could be considered to be a disability based on the significance of the impact a handicap has on a person.

II. The **Age Discrimination in Employment Act** (ADEA) prevents an employer from discriminating against applicants or employees who are 40 years of age or older as pertains to hiring, job transfers or promotions, wages, benefits, layoffs, training or further job education, firing or other conditions that may fall under their employment.

ADEA does not apply if employers discriminate because they feel an individual under 40 years old is not old enough or well suited enough for a position.

III. Under Title VII of the **Civil Rights Act of 1964**, any employer who has fifteen or more employees may not discriminate against an employment candidate or employee based on skin color, gender, national origin, pregnancy, race, religious beliefs or practices or sexual orientation.

IV. The **Clayton Antitrust Act** defines unethical business practices. In addition to that, the law makes provisions to regulate business practices; places bans on anticompetitive mergers, price discrimination and unethical behavior by companies; protects individuals who experience violations to their rights by companies and gives employees the right to protest to that end.

V. The **Consolidated Omnibus Budget Reconciliation Act** (COBRA) grants employees the choice to keep their health insurance coverage when it would typically be lost due to temporary layoffs, job loss, hour cutbacks, changes or transitions in a job, the death of a parent or spouse or other disruptive life events. The events that are covered under COBRA allow individuals to choose to keep their health benefits for a set period of time.

Generally speaking, the insurance in question is most often part of an employee group health plan, and if an individual chooses to keep the insurance during this time, he or she must pay for part or all of the premium for the duration. An example of COBRA would be an employee taking FMLA to have surgery. During the person's time off work, while the employee isn't earning a paycheck, he or she may choose to pay the premiums while on leave. When the employee returns to work, and the insurance is once again taken out of the person's paycheck, the individual will no longer pay for premiums out of pocket.

VI. The **Consumer Credit Protection Act** is a federal law that protects consumers against lenders. The law requires that lenders reveal the actual cost of borrowing funds. Furthermore, the terms must be stated plainly in a way that the customers can understand. The Consumer Credit Protection Act has been amended since it was initially enacted in 1968 to include the Truth in Lending Act, Title III and the Fair Credit Reporting Act.

VII. The **Dodd-Frank Wall Street Reform and Consumer Protection Act**, better known as just the Dodd-Frank Act, was designed to make publicly traded companies comply with compensation practices. These practices require that a public company provide disclosure and include shareholder voting rights. This law authorizes the Securities and Exchange Commission to make rules and requirements including but not limited to shareholder disclosure, approval of golden parachutes, say on pay and say on pay frequency.

The law was created as a means for creating financial stability, making improvements to the accountability of publicly traded companies, creating levels of transparency and stopping bailouts supported by taxpayer dollars.

VIII. The **Employee Retirement Income Security Act** (ERISA) was enacted to ensure that the money individuals put into a retirement plan during their working lives is guaranteed to be there at retirement. Minimum standards must be met by employers or private retirement plan holders.

The Department of Labor is responsible for applying and protecting the provisions made under ERISA. The act does not require any employer to establish a pension plan for employees. It just outlines what requirements must be met by those who do establish such plans and sets the rules to ensure that the money placed in a pension plan is kept secure.

IX. The **Employment Polygraph Protection Act** bans the majority of employers from using lie detector tests as a part of their hiring process. While there are some select employers who are exempt from this law, it applies to the bulk of employers. The law prohibits most employers from requiring or even requesting that employment candidates or employees undergo a lie detector test. Furthermore, this law mandates that employees cannot be fired, suffer disciplinary action or be discriminated against in regard to hiring.

X. The **Equal Pay Act** was enacted to outlaw wage discrimination based on an individual's sex as a means of building earning equity between men and women who work in the same fields, hold the same qualifications, have similar working conditions and put in the same or similar efforts.

XI. The **Family and Medical Leave Act** (FMLA) accords job protection for all employees who work a minimum of 1,250 hours in a twelve-month period if they need to take leave for family or medical reasons. While on leave, employees are granted continued group health insurance that they would usually receive through their employers.

To qualify for provisions under the FMLA, individuals must work for a company that has at least 50 employees, located within 75 miles of their employer. These qualifications, even when met, still offer some specific exclusions to those stipulations.

FMLA allows qualified employees to take up to twelve weeks off for their own personal medical reasons or for immediate family. The twelve weeks work on a rolling calendar schedule. Specialty provisions are made for intermittent use of FMLA for those who need such concessions as well.

XII. The **Fair Credit Reporting Act** was enacted as a way to regulate and protect consumer information. The Federal Trade Commission is responsible for the collection, distribution and use of consumer information. The FCRA mandates that the use of personal information gathered by credit reporting organizations is treated in a fair, accurate and private manner. It also requires that any person or organization that requests information contained in an individual's credit report must prove they are permitted to request and receive such information by law before that information is shared.

For a consumer report to be issued to an employer, written consent must be given by an applicant or employee. The consent form must clearly state whose information is being requested, why and what specific information is being requested.

XIII. The **Fair Labor Standards Act** (FLSA) sets the minimum wage and pay for overtime work and regulates child labor. Additionally, the FLSA defines what employees are covered under the law, as well as outlining those that are exempt from its application. Work hours that are covered under the FLSA include but are not limited to training, meetings and on-call hours. Also included in the FLSA are work-related travel time, legally required rest periods, work-related waiting periods, work- or business-related meals and legally mandated breaks.

XIV. The **Federal Employment Compensation Act** sets the law for federal workers to receive benefits and compensation in the event that they are injured on the job. The provisions under the law state that the injured employee will receive coverage for medical expenses, compensation for any loss in wages and provides payments to federal employees' dependents in the event that they die because of a work-related illness or injury.

XV. The **Federal Insurance Contributions Act** legally established the taxes that fund Medicare and Social Security. The law requires that employers withdraw the right amount for Medicare and Social Security from employee paychecks and submit it to the proper government agencies.

XVI. The **Federal Unemployment Tax Act** allocates money paid by employees, collected by employers and then given to the state to fund unemployment. The money is put into the unemployment fund as a means of paying eligible claims for unemployment insurance.

XVII. The **Genetic Information Nondiscrimination Act** (GINA) was enacted to prevent any health insurance companies and health plans from denying individuals health coverage or upcharging individuals on health-care coverage because of genetic predisposition to illness. GINA means that anyone that has a genetic predisposition to developing a health issue later in life but is an otherwise healthy person can't be prevented from getting health-care coverage or be charged more money for coverage.

GINA further prevents an employer from using genetic information in regard to making decisions on hiring or firing employees, transferring jobs or advancing an individual's career ladder. These mandates are enforced by the Equal Employment Opportunity Commission (EEOC).

XVIII. The **Health Insurance Portability and Accountability Act (HIPAA)** was enacted to protect the confidentiality and security of individuals' health information. HIPAA requires health-care providers to develop procedures within their organizations that protect health-care information that is transferred, received or otherwise handled by those providers.

The protection enforced under this law is further used to aid in reducing the chances of personal medical information being misused. The law applies to hard copies of information as well as electronic medical information, and it requires proper shredding when disposing of this information.

XIX. The **Immigration and Nationality Act** pertains to all immigration-related issues as they apply to employment. The law was first enacted to prevent any employer from discriminating against employment candidates and employees because of their immigration status. It makes provisions in the United States for aliens regarding both temporary and permanent employment. Finally, the Immigration and Nationality Act requires employers to have all employment candidates and employees complete the I-9 form to verify their eligibility to work in the United States.

XX. The **Labor Management Reporting and Disclosure Act** was enacted in order to protect the money and assets of labor organizations.

XXI. The **Longshore and Harbor Workers' Compensation Act** is a federal law that covers the medical care and compensation of those who work in US waters, harbors or wherever water vessels are built, repaired, loaded or unloaded. The law specifically states that any employee injured while on such a job will receive wage compensation, coverage of medical expenses and rehabilitation. Furthermore, the law requires that dependents of injured or deceased employees receive survivors' benefits.

XXII. The **National Labor Relations Act** was enacted to define employer and employee rights. These rights include, but are not limited to, the right to bargain, participate in strikes, file grievances or otherwise seek aid or negotiate. This law allows both employers and employees to rectify unfair wages or compensation, unsafe working conditions or other such grievances.

XXIII. The **Ohio Pregnancy Discrimination Act** is an administrative code under Ohio law that pertains to pregnant women and extends to childbirth. This law applies only to the state of Ohio and was enacted to apply to businesses and organizations, including those that do not fall under the coverage of FMLA. The Ohio Pregnancy Discrimination Act, known as Administrative Code Chapter 4112-5-05 (G), entitles female employees to what is considered to be a "reasonable" period of time for pregnancy and childbirth leave. At the end of this designated leave, the employee must be reinstated to the position that she originally had, or an employer must give her a position that has the same status and salary. Furthermore, the employee is not allowed to lose any seniority or other such benefits due to her time away for pregnancy, childbirth or postpartum recovery.

XXIV. The **Occupational Safety and Health Act** (OSHA) was enacted for the main purpose of federally regulating health and safety in the workplace. The Department of Labor is responsible for tracking and inspecting workplaces to ensure their compliance with OSHA. OSHA makes sure that employers are providing all employees with a work environment that is free of hazards to individual or group health.

These hazards include but are not limited to toxic chemicals, excessive levels of noise, mechanical or machine-related dangers and excessive exposure to hot or cold temperatures or unsanitary conditions. In the event that the job directly puts employees in harm's way, such as working with toxic chemicals, working around heavy machinery or cleaning unsanitary work sites, employers are then required to provide employees with personal protective equipment that appropriately protects them from the conditions of their work. These protections can include but are not limited to safety glasses, hazmat suits, protective gloves and waterproof rubberized boots or suits.

XXV. The **Patent Act** was enacted to protect the inventions of those who secure a patent, which prohibits others from producing, using or selling their invention without explicit permission. The act is overseen by the Patent and Trademark Office.

XXVI. The **Patient Protection and Affordable Care Act** (PPACA), best known as Obamacare, was enacted to expand health-care coverage. It uses both public health insurance and private health insurance to expand health-care coverage and makes provisions to expand the eligibility for coverage under both Medicaid and Medicare. Additionally, it sets a variety of other health-care standards.

By law, through Obamacare, all individuals must purchase health-care insurance, and all employers who employ 50 or more employees must offer health insurance coverage to their employees. Failure of qualified employers to offer health insurance coverage will face financial penalties.

XXVII. The **Portal-to-Portal Act** was enacted to ensure that employees receive payment for all of the time they work.

XXVIII. The **Pregnancy Discrimination Act** prevents employers from discriminating against employment candidates or employees based on any pregnancy-related conditions. An exclusion to this law is any woman who has an elective abortion, in which case there is no protection under the Pregnancy Discrimination Act.

XXIX. The **Public Contracts Act** was enacted and amended in order to set the legal guidelines for contract work. The law sets the standard for any contract work that is $15,000 or greater and sets the term for minimum wage as it applies to contracted work. The act also outlines the maximum number of hours on a contract and sets the standards for health and safety in contracted work.

XXX. The **Railway Labor Act** was enacted to resolve disputes in the airline and railway industries. The law uses arbitration, mediation and bargaining in lieu of labor strikes to solve any workplace disputes.

XXXI. The **Sarbanes-Oxley Act** was enacted in 2020 and is otherwise known as the Public Company Accounting Reform and Investor Protection Act or Corporate and Auditing Accountabilities, Responsibilities Kind and Transparency Act. The act ensures that large companies and corporations use a more transparent approach by requiring them to disclose accurate information to investors.

The law requires clear financial statements, without false statements or omissions, honestly representing a company's financial health. Companies must also provide a list of any deficits. Furthermore, companies are required to publish detailed annual reports that show internal controls are working correctly. Companies are legally mandated to let their investors and shareholders know immediately if there are any major changes to the corporation's finances. This includes but is not limited to operations, acquisitions, divestments and major staff changes.

Anyone in these corporations who fails to comply with the law will be prosecuted, and if found guilty, could face up to 20 years in prison. Failing to comply is defined as concealing, destroying or changing any records or documentation regarding financial statements, impeding investigations or otherwise interfering or lying about the company's financial state.

XXXII. The **Service Contract Act** legally requires that contractors and subcontractors that are working on contracts equal or greater to $2,500 pay a wage to those performing the services that is at least equal to or greater than the wages that are common to that area at the time that the service is being conducted.

XXXIII. The **Sherman Antitrust Act** was enacted as a way to prevent monopolies in business. Unlike many local or state laws on the subject, the Sherman Antitrust Act applies to interstate commerce throughout the United States.

XXXIV. The **Social Security Act** was enacted to protect and provide for aging and vulnerable populations in the United States, including the elderly, blind and those with disabilities. It provides for child and maternal welfare and public health. It further establishes and manages unemployment benefits and compensation while also establishing a social security board to raise money for such funding.

XXXV. The **Uniformed Services Employment and Reemployment Rights Act** was enacted in order to protect service members from being discriminated against because of their status as members of the United States military. The law is regulated by the Veterans' Employment and Training Service.

The law requires that service members who are deployed, leave for basic, leave for their scheduled training or are otherwise pulled away from work for military service must be reinstated to the same job that they previously held. They must also receive the same pay and benefits they had when they left. Additionally, they will receive any job promotions, seniority raises, additional benefits and other compensation that they would have received if they had not left for military duty.

XXXVI. The **Worker Adjustment and Retraining Notification Act** is overseen by the Department of Labor. The law was enacted to protect workers, the families of workers and their communities in the event of a business closing or having major layoffs. The law provides these protections by mandating that any business operating a plant with at least 100 employees or more notify employees no less than 60 days before a plant has any massive layoffs or if a plant is scheduled to close. The only exceptions to this 60-day law are in the event that a business has an unforeseeable situation or is affected by a natural disaster. In the event that those circumstances arise, then the employer is not required to give any notice at all.

Important Agencies Human Resources Personnel Should Know

Human resources personnel should be familiar with the organizations that are responsible for making sure that a business is complying with local, state and federal laws and regulations as they pertain to hiring, employing, firing or otherwise relate to individuals within a company's employment.

These organizations are important for several reasons. They ensure the fair hiring and firing of individuals. They also ensure the overall safety and welfare of employers and employees. Finally, they ensure that organizations are in compliance with documents, signage, insurance and other similar points throughout a business.

- Department of Labor (DOL)
    - The United States Department of Labor is an organization of the federal government responsible for setting and enforcing the standard wage, unemployment insurance, reemployment services, occupational safety and more.
- Employee Benefits Security Administration (ESBA)
    - The Employee Benefits Security Administration is responsible for administering, regulating and enforcing the terms that are covered under Title I of the Employee Retirement Income Security Act.
- Equal Employment Opportunity Commission (EEOC)
    - The United States Equal Employment Opportunity Commission is a federally regulated agency that regulates and enforces laws relating to civil rights as they pertain to discrimination in the workplace.
- Federal Trade Commission
    - The Federal Trade Commission is a government organization responsible for enforcing antitrust laws. It is also tasked with promoting consumer protections.
- International Labor Organization
    - The International Labor Organization advances work opportunities in an attempt to provide good working conditions that are

conducive to freedom, equality, security and human dignity for men and women internationally.

- Merit System Protection Board
    - The United States Merit System Protection Board is tasked with the responsibility of protecting federal merit systems by preventing specific individuals from violating the system through the abuse of power and by protecting federal employees of the United States.
- National Labor Relations Board
    - The National Labor Relations Board is responsible for the enforcement of labor laws in the United States as they relate to unfair labor practices.
- Occupational Safety and Health Administration (OSHA)
    - OSHA is responsible for ensuring the safety and health of the workplace.
- Securities and Exchange Commission
    - The Securities and Exchange Commission is a federal organization responsible for the orderly functioning of the securities market.
- U.S. Commission on Civil Rights
    - The United States Commission on Civil Rights is responsible for investigating and reporting any concerns within an organization as they pertain to civil rights.
- U.S. Department of Justice – Division of Civil Rights
    - The Civil Rights Division of the United States Department of Justice is a branch of the Justice Department and is responsible for enforcing laws against those who discriminate based on disability, gender, national origin, race or religion.
- Veterans' Employment Training Service
    - The United States Veterans' Employment Training Service is a program developed to help military veterans gain the education that they require to enter or reenter the workforce.

Key Terms, Models and Business Structures to Know in the Field of Human Resources

A:

- Ability-to-pay factors
    - Incentive programs
    - Internal conditions
    - Total rewards programs

- Absentee rates – the number of days absent versus the number of days worked an individual has over a set time period.

- Acceptance of risk – when individuals, businesses or organizations acknowledge that there is a possibility of risk, however, that risk is low enough that a business determines the venture is worth taking the risk and assumes the responsibility if it fails.

- Accession rate – employees added to the payroll over a given period of time. This number is then presented in the form of a percentage.

- Accidental death and dismemberment insurance – insurance that covers employers and employees that are on the job in the event of a work-related injury or death. Such insurance will cover medical expenses, physical or occupational therapy, lost wages, pay benefits to dependents, etc.

- Accommodation requests under the ADA – the document that officially requests that accommodations be made by an employer to allow a disabled employee to effectively do his/her job.

- Accounting for employees in emergency action plans – a plan that is developed by employers for what should occur in the event of an emergency. The plan includes a method of ensuring that every employee can be accounted for should such an emergency arise.

- Accrual – an accounting method that highlights the financials of an organization by using the income generated and the expenses, organizes any income and expenses and then compares that to the invoices that have been paid or to the payments the organization has received.

- Accrual requirements in ERISA – designed to protect employee benefits plans, their beneficiaries and their overall interests.

- Acquired needs theory – the needs of an individual as they pertain to life experience, knowledge gained, achievements made and affiliations.

- Acquiring company – an organization purchasing another company.

- Acquisition – an acquisition refers to the purchase of a business.

- Action plans – a plan of action or strategy.

- ADDIE model – ADDIE is an acronym for a five-step training model that uses analysis, design, development, implementation and evaluation. The first step is to analyze, which means to review the current business model and how it is working. The company determines the long-term goals it has for its future.

  Next, with that information, the company builds a training plan that will help the organization achieve these goals by understanding:

  1. Who the company is training

2. What the company wants to achieve
3. When the organization wants to achieve it
4. Why those goals are important to reach
5. How the business can be helped to reach these goals.

Designing a training plan may include:

- Strategizing
- Selecting the best delivery method for the target audience being trained
- Determining the appropriate length of training for that situation
- Assessing the overall needs of the training
- Collecting feedback to ensure effectiveness
- Adjusting key points as needed.

With these steps complete, HR will create a training course based on all of the data and information collected. The course will be implemented and then evaluated to ensure that it is working to adequately meet the long-term goals of the organization in question.

- Ad hoc – an off-the-cuff solution for an unforeseen situation that cannot be prepared for in advance or predicted before it occurs.

- Alternative dispute resolution – a way of resolving a disagreement between two or more parties that allows for the issued to be settled in a way that does not utilize formal legal proceedings.

Administrative exemptions – jobs that are excluded from certain rights and protections under the FLSA. These include minimum wage and overtime regulations.

- Adverse impact calculators – a way in which hiring, promotions and other decisions regarding employment are made.

- Advocacy – to give support on behalf of another. In reference to HR, advocacy most often refers to supporting an individual, cause or idea by assisting with the overall outcome in a specific situation.

- Advice of counsel clause in employment contracts – an employee or potential employee advised to seek legal counsel prior to signing an employment contract or promotion contract.

- Affirmative action – a process that is applied to all employment applicants as a means of treating them equally.

- All-hands staff meeting – refers to all employees being gathered for a staff meeting. These meetings are used to ensure that all of the employees of a company are given the same information at the same time.

- Alliance – an agreement that happens between parties to allow both sides of the partnership to benefit mutually.

- Allowance – money provided to an individual for a given purpose. Most often, allowances are given to an employee as compensation for a work-related expense.

- Alternative dispute resolution – the use of mediation or arbitration to resolve a dispute as opposed to litigation.

- American Arbitration Association (AAA) – a nonprofit group that resolves issues using methods other than litigation.

- Angoff Method – a process that uses experts to determine the likelihood of a candidate choosing the correct answer on an employment entrance exam. The likelihood of the average exam score is then used to set a standard.

- Analysis tools – a set of resources used to collect information to improve workforce performance. This is done by gathering data that supports effective plans and outlining areas that need improvement.

- Annual reports – a yearly financial report that is provided to shareholders or other investors.

- Annual reviews – a review of an employee's performance, generally done on an annual basis to determine raises and assess the potential for promotions.

- Appeal – an official method afforded to employees or organizations that allows them to challenge an official decision that has been made in the workplace or business setting. This allows the conclusions to be reviewed by the appropriate authorities and opens the door for a possible change to the original ruling or decision.

- Application tracking system – a computer software system that assists HR departments, team leaders, organizations and employment recruiters in tracking applications.

- Appraisal – a survey used to assess value or performance. Generally used to find an organization's overall value.

- Apprentice – a term applied to individuals who are learning a skill, trade or profession by watching a trained professional and practicing their own skills under supervision. Apprentices are most often found in careers including but not limited to plumbing, carpentry, mechanics and construction.

- Arbitration – a legal process that allows parties involved in a legal matter to jointly waive their right to a jury trial in order to go directly before a judge as a means of arriving at a speedy outcome. Typically, the judge's ruling is final, and no further action can be taken regarding the matter once the ruling is made.

- Assignment and assignee – an assignment refers to a job or position that is not in an individual's typical employment zone. Most often, the assignee is an employee who is working abroad.

- Asynchronous learning – a teaching or training method that utilizes online learning to instruct students and employees. This particular type of teaching is designed to facilitate the instruction of pupils who may be in different time zones from instructors.

- Attrition – the process by which a business undergoes a reduction in the number of employees it has either through the end of an employment contract, employee resignation, illness, death, retirement or termination.

B:

- Background check – completed for a variety of reasons including but not limited to vetting individuals for employment, confirming employment history, clearing individuals for employment by confirming criminal history and vetting employees for security clearances.

- Back wages recovery – wages that an employer owes to an employee. Back wage recovery is the payment of those unpaid or "back-pay" wages.

- Balance-sheet approach – a model used to standardize salary, benefits and compensation for individuals who work internationally.

- Balanced scorecard – the planning and management system used to convey an individual's intended accomplishments.

- Base pay – the pay rate for a job before any additional money or compensation, such as bonuses or overtime.

- Base salary – the set starting pay for a job, excluding benefits, bonuses, commissions or other compensation.

- Behavioral interview – an interview technique that uses the past work history of employment candidates and/or current employees to gauge candidates' or employees' future job performance.

- Benchmark positions in job evaluation processes – jobs with a standard set of responsibilities and a steady and reliable salary.

- Beneficiary – a person, group or organization that is assigned to receive the benefits as part of a retirement plan, insurance policy or will.

- Benefit program – a combination of benefits that may include but is not limited to health insurance, dental insurance, vision insurance, short-term disability, long-term disability, life insurance, retirement plans and stock options offered to employees.

- Benefits – can refer to any compensation given to an employee that is not cash. This can include but is not limited to health insurance, dental insurance, vision insurance, short-term disability, long-term disability, life insurance, retirement plans, stock options, allowances for housing or clothing, company meals, memberships to recreational clubs, company housing, allowances for housing or moving expenses or any other similar options given to an employee in addition to the standard salary.

- Bereavement leave – up to three days of paid leave offered to employees who experience the death of an immediate family member (*immediate* being defined by the employer).

- Best practices – a proven way of getting the best results for an organization.

- Biodata (biological data) – the education, work history and background that is collected on any given individual.

- Blackout period – a business term that is used to refer to a time when employees are denied the ability to make changes or allowed access to particular plans, benefits or compensation such as their retirement plans or stock options.

- Blended learning – refers to a type of training or continued education that allows instructors to blend in-class instruction and e-learning when training employees.

- Boycotts – to stop patronizing an individual, organization or business.

- Breakdown analysis – the process of organizing the sources of revenue and other important aspects of an organization.

- Briefing – a method used by HR departments and members of management to disperse information throughout a business. More specifically, it is a way of sharing information with potential employment candidates, employees and anyone else associated with an establishment.

- Business impact measures – a set of standards that are put in place to evaluate the impact on a business.

- Business process outsource – subcontracting or outsourcing to a third-party vendor.

- Buy-in – a term that refers to other individuals or groups investing money into an organization. It is ultimately a sponsorship for the business. It can be a permanent partnership, or it can be a temporary assist until the buy-in terms have been repaid, and the business can stand on its own.

C:

- Callback pay – pay that is earned by employees when they are required to go back to work for an emergency after they have already punched out or taken leave.

- Candidate selection tools – a tool for selecting candidates that includes interviewing, skills testing, psychological evaluations and reference checks, among other things.

- Capital budgets – when money is set aside for maintenance in order to fix things like buildings or equipment, or for the purpose of acquisitions and purchases.

- Career development – the process individuals follow to progress in their professional careers. This can include but is not limited to continuing training and education, applying for and accepting career advancements and moving into higher positions.

- Career ladder promotions – refers to moving the next step up the professional ladder. For example, an employee may start as an entry-level receptionist. That employee may then be promoted to personal secretary for a team leader or department manager, then he/she may move up to an administrative assistant for upper management. Finally, that employee may become an executive administrative assistant for the company CEO.

- Career management – the process of planning and pursuing professional development and advancement. Many times, there is an individual within HR that helps employees to strategize the career path they envision and plan how to take advantage of training, education and skills to help people develop and advance within their chosen field.

- Career planning – the setting of professional goals, outlining how to reach those goals and the steps taken to reach each set goal in a timely and efficient manner.

- Career plateau – a time in an individual's career when a person has stalled out because of a lack of continued education or has reached a peak in the career field and must choose to either stay put or change career lanes. It can also mean a time when there are simply no other advancement opportunities within a company or job field.

- Career portfolios – an in-depth analysis of an individual's employment history and career accomplishments. A career portfolio most often consists of employees' work history, skills gained over the course of their career, accomplishments and any other pertinent information.

- Cash balance plan – most often refers to a pension plan savings account, allowing for lifetime annuity payments.

- Caux principles – a set of international ethical guidelines for organizations. These guidelines were created by the Caux Round Table, which is a group of global business leaders who create guidelines and standards for the ethical and responsible business dealings of international organizations.

- Certification – a certificate or degree that is issued to individuals or an organization to accredit them for having passed a certain exam that reflects on their professional abilities.

- Chain of command – the organized structure of authority within a business. It can be looked at from the bottom up or from the top down. An example of the chain of command within a business would be: The chief executive officer (CEO) is the highest executive in a business, the person in charge. Below the CEO might be the vice president, followed by the director of operations, then senior managers, department managers, team leaders and finally, team members (entry-level employees).

- Change agent – an agent that works with an organization in order to help improve its overall effectiveness and development.

- Chemical health hazards – chemicals such as carcinogens, toxic agents, irritants, corrosives, sensitizers, neurotoxins and other such agents and solutions that can cause damage to the lungs, skin, eyes or other body parts.

- Child labor provisions – United States' federal child labor laws under the FLSA that prohibit children from being employed in what is considered to be oppressive labor.

- Cliff vesting – when employees fully own a plan all at once rather than staggering it over a period of time.

- Cloud computing – a method utilized by many organizations in which all of an organization's sharable content is put on a group of servers. This method uses the convenience and flexibility of the internet to create an online network that can be accessed, managed and shared with anyone within an organization to share information securely.

- Coaching – a method of training, education and support that is sometimes used within a business to support employees.

- Code of ethics – an organization's outline of what is and is not allowed in regard to employee behaviors.

- Collective bargaining agreement – a written contract that is entered into by a union and an employer. Such an agreement contractually obligates those who enter the contract together to terms regarding wages, overtime, bonuses, seniority, layoffs, termination, discipline and more.

- Commission – a salary or pay that is based on sales or a percentage rather than hours worked.

- Common law employment – the legal term that refers to an employment arrangement where employees are required to do the job by the terms the employer sets.

- Communication skills – the skills of listening, body language, eye contact, hand gestures, clarity, empathy, respect and other such forms of communication.

- Comparable worth – the rates of pay for women and men in similar fields.

- Compensatory time off – compensatory pay is paid time off given to employees as compensation for overtime hours worked.

- Compliance – ensuring that a business, organization or employees are following company guidelines and policies, as well as state and federal laws.

- Consolidation – the process of combining or paring down of resources within a business. This can mean combining multiple companies that are owned by a parent company to eliminate redundancies such as multiple HR departments, streamlining production lines, combining assets, consolidating resources and otherwise limiting liabilities to improve the overall success and efficiency of an organization.

- Contingent worker – an individual's employment that has a set time frame. For example, a contingent worker may be an individual who was hired for the holiday season while there was a surplus of work, contracted employees who are hired for a defined period of time or employees who are hired with a definite end date at the time they are hired. These employees will leave at the end of that set time frame unless another contracted time frame is negotiated and agreed upon.

- Continuous FMLA – FMLA leave that is not separated by periods of work, but rather is ongoing.

- Contract bias – when a contract between two parties is more in favor of one party than the other.

- Contract manufacturing – a specific method of producing goods involving hiring an outside company to do part or all of the production for a specific product. For example, say a company builds children's bikes. The bike tires take longer to produce than the bike frame. At Christmas, the company hires an outside manufacturer to produce the bike tires because the manufacturer's facility can produce two tires in the time it takes for the host company to build one frame. This allows the company to keep up production with the orders throughout the busy holiday season.

- Corporate citizenship – when a business helps positively impact the community it is located in.

- Corporate culture – the values, rules, processes, procedures and expectations a business has. This includes the organization's behavior, the expectations that organization has for its employees' conduct and the way that the organization is viewed by the world.

- Corporate governance – rules, processes and regulations that dictate the running of a business.

- Corporate restructuring – the changing of the way an organization is structured and operates.

- Corporate social responsibility – pertains to the environmental and community commitments that a business makes to the communities it is located in. Those responsibilities can be environmental or social and refer to a whole community's well-being.

- Cost-benefit analysis– an important tool for any organization to be successful. A cost-benefit analysis is a way of comparing information. Specifically, it compares the cost of a business decision at start-up, what that decision will cost to keep it going and what kind of revenue it will create. The point of a cost-benefit analysis is most often to ensure that the cost of a venture will be outweighed by the revenue it generates. For example, Fine Wines decides to open a vineyard closer to its factory. The vineyard will cost half a million dollars to cultivate the land, build facilities, purchase equipment and so on. Additionally, it will cost Fine Wine $25,000 each year to run the business after the initial investment is paid back. By building the new vineyard, the company will no longer have to lease the land it is currently growing grapes on and will save over $75,000 a year by not having to ship grapes in. If the venture is successful, the vineyard will generate one million dollars or more a year in revenue for the Fine Wine company.

A cost-benefit analysis would show that while it will cost a large sum of money to get the vineyard off the ground, the company will save more money by owning its own vineyard, not having to lease land and cutting the cost of having to ship grapes in.

- Cost of living adjustment – an adjustment to the pay that an employee receives strictly based on the economy in the person's location and the cost to live there.

- Cost per hire – a recruitment tool that assists employers and HR departments in determining the budget needed to recruit employees to a given company. The cost per hire model works by calculating the cost to advertise for a job, the fees associated with recruiting employees, the fees to be paid for any referrals and travel expense reimbursements, to name just some of the costs associated with hiring.

- Credentials – the certification of an individual's credentials. This proof can come in the form of a certificate, diploma, digital badge or other similar proof that documents an individual or organization's skills, training, etc.

- Criterion – a standardized reference used to confirm that an individual has completed a specific requirement in order to meet a minimum standard. An example of a criterion would be an employee who is required to obtain a certification, associate degree, bachelor's degree or master's degree in order to meet the minimum standards to be accepted for a position within a company.

- Cross-border business – business that is conducted across international boundaries between at least two countries. An example of cross-border business is Walmart, which does business in the United States, Canada, Mexico and several other countries internationally.

- Cross-training – a practice in which a business trains employees not only for the job they do on a daily basis but also to do another job within the organization. For example, say a cashier works on the front end of a retail store. Management decides to also train her in how to unload trucks in the back and check in merchandise that arrives. They also train her on how to scan the merchandise and put it out on the floor. Therefore, the employee has been cross-trained to work in up to three positions throughout the store. If the store makes cutbacks or an employee in one of these areas is out sick, that employee can now fill any of these three positions. Cross-training can save companies money by eliminating the need to hire a temporary employee, or in the event that a company needs to make cutbacks, it now has an existing employee that can work multiple positions.

- Cultural coaching – a training technique that organizations utilize for educating employees about the cultural differences that they may encounter while conducting business. The training allows for smoother business practices. An example of cultural coaching would be educating a group of American employees on the cultural differences they will encounter with the Korean company they will be meeting with as part of a business merger over the next several months.

- Cultural intelligence – an individual's ability to understand and operate in multicultural environments so as not to cause offense.

- Customer service representative – an individual who advises and interacts with customers as pertains to resolving conflicts, processing orders, providing information and otherwise assisting customers.

D:

- Danger premium – a higher rate of pay or pay in addition to an individual's typical salary for doing high-risk work or working in a high-risk area. High risk specifically means when individuals are given more money because their lives are put in imminent peril because of the location they are working in. An example would be someone who is sent to work in the Congo receiving an additional $1,000 a week because the Congo is an incredibly dangerous area to work in. By taking the position there, the employee is risking being shot, kidnapped or sold into slavery, among other things.

- Data collection – gathering information on a given topic, person or organization, organizing the information and drawing conclusions based upon it.

- Days to fill – the amount of time that it takes for HR to fill a vacant position within an organization.

- Debt garnishment – a method of obtaining a court order in which debts can be deducted from an employee's paycheck and paid to the debtor before the employee receives the remainder of his/her wages.

- Decline stage – when the life cycle of a product drops. In other words, it is the drop in sales on a given product.

- Dedicated HR or dedicated HR personnel – an individual that works strictly in the HR department and does not work outside of that specific job function.

- Deferred compensation plan – an employee retirement or pension program that lets employees who have put money into that retirement fund over the life of their career take that money out in one payment or lump sum when they retire. The money in this type of retirement or pension plan is not taxed until it is withdrawn. This is often seen as a good thing because many individuals pay a lower tax at the time of retirement than they would have if the money had been taxed when it was first put into the plan.

- Defined benefits plan – a pension plan that has a set payment schedule upon retirement. When signing up for the plan, employees are told up front what the payment amount and payment schedule will be upon retirement. Policy holders have the option to either receive the total amount in one single payment upon retirement or to arrange for the payments to be made on a payment schedule such as biweekly, monthly, semiannually or annually.

- Department staff meeting – when all of the employees within a given department of a business are expected to show up for a meeting regarding that department. It allows all of the staff in the department to receive the same information, all at the same time.

- Disaster recovery plan – a written document that outlines the approach a business will take to get operations back on track after a disaster.

- Disposable earnings – the amount of money that is left for employees after local, state and federal governments have deducted the legally allowed amount.

- Distance learning – a way of training employees by using methods of remote learning. This can include but is not limited to using TV, tapes, DVDs, videos, computers, the internet and YouTube in order to get instructional materials across. Distance learning can also be a combination of traditional in-class instruction and alternative methods.

- Distributed training – a method used by businesses that stretches out the training process over extended periods of time. Training may be done in a variety of locations and may be instituted using a wide array of methods.

This employee training method works by allowing employees to absorb smaller amounts of information and ways of doing things without overwhelming them.

- Distributive bargaining – the negotiation style shares the distribution of assets between all parties involved.

- Diversity – having variety and different things to offer.

- Document retention – federal laws mandate the retention of some documents for a distinct period of time. There can also be local, state or country laws that require document retention for a business.

- Domestic partnership – the relationship between two or more individuals, parties, businesses or organizations that work or live together in an effort to share resources and benefit jointly.

- Downsizing – any time a business reduces the number of employees it has. Downsizing can be done for a variety of reasons, including but not limited to streamlining processes, creating a more efficient workflow, ensuring the profitability of a business, cutting out overstaffing, etc.

- Due diligence for mergers – analyzing a commercial entity carefully before purchasing it. Most commonly done in the process of closing on a merger, acquisition or other such purchase or investment.

E:

- Economic valuation – a way of assigning a financial value to things that would otherwise not have one. This is done by reviewing the environmental factors of an organization and determining a realistic value for those things. These factors may include things such as air quality, water quality and carbon emissions. Once such factors have received a valuation, that value can then be added to the financial value of a business to increase its overall worth.

- Effective interviews – the main point of such interviews is to ascertain an individual's skill level, education level, background and other such abilities as they pertain to work and employment.

- Elder-care benefits – these benefits assist employers in reducing caregiver stress on employees. They ensure that loved ones and family members are well taken care of while employees are at work. This benefit offers employees a good sense of work-life balance.

- E-learning – a method utilized by businesses as a means of training staff. The e-learning approach often lends the most flexibility to both the business and the staff. It generally utilizes a tracking system that can monitor an individual's progress and determine when a person has successfully completed the course or materials, without the need to hire an instructor.

- Emergency risk assessment – assessing the risks in an emergency, disaster or crisis.

- Emergency action plan – a written document designed to facilitate and organize actions taken by employers and employees in the event of an emergency in the workplace. OSHA standards require that an emergency action plan be on hand and kept up to date.

- Employee and labor relations – the preventing and/or resolving of problems between employees in a work situation.

- Employee assistance program – a program that some businesses utilize that assists employees with personal issues related to their lives outside of work, but that can affect their work performance and productivity. Employee assistance programs offer things such as support, counseling services and addiction or rehab services to employees and their families to help them through their personal issues with the hopes of keeping them at work or helping them to return to work in the healthiest way possible.

- Employee benefits – refers to the non-salaried benefits afforded to an employee by an organization. These benefits may include dental insurance, vision insurance, pension or retirement plans, reimbursements for employees' continuing education, allowances for transportation or clothing, housing allowances or moving expenses.

- Employee handbook – a compilation of a business' benefits, codes of conduct, compensation, policies and procedures. This may be compiled into a few documents, a manual or a book. Employee handbooks or manuals most often contain a signature page in which employees can ascertain that they have read and understood the contents.

- Employee referrals – when an employment candidate has been recommended or referred by an employee who is already employed by the organization.

- Employee relations – an essential component of the HR department. Employee relations is all about communication from the top of an organization to the bottom and from the bottom all the way back up to the top. Communicating is the key component in conflict resolution, complying with policies, regulations, laws, developing careers, helping employees to move up their respective career ladders and measuring performance and development.

- Employee retention – an important aspect of any business. Employee retention requires employees to feel satisfied in their job and to be fairly compensated in their work.

- Employee rights and responsibilities – an employee's legal rights, statutory rights and responsibilities.

- Employee self-service – a method utilized by HR departments that allows employees and staff members to access their employer's database containing their personal employment, benefits and compensation information. While not all information will be accessible or editable, the employee self-service system allows employees and staff to log into their information and update personal data. This data can include things such as home address, phone number, email address, emergency contacts, basic medical information, spouse and dependents.

- Employee stock ownership plan – a retirement plan in which stocks are contributed by the company of employment.

- Employee turnover – the rate at which employees leave an organization, the number of unfilled positions and the time it takes to fill vacancies at any given time within the business.

- Employer branding – the way in which a business represents itself to the community and the public through outreach, branding, employee satisfaction, stockholders and customers.

- Employer-paid benefits – benefits provided to employees and staff of a business, in addition to the employee or staff members' regular salary, at the employer's expense.

- Employment at will – the United States' legal definition of a working relationship between staff or employees of a business and their relationship with their employers.

- Employment branding – a business' efforts to improve public perception of the enterprise. The organization makes an active effort to make changes to become what is known as an "employer of choice." The improvement to branding is done in an attempt to attract qualified employees and retain already highly qualified employees.

- Employment practices liability insurance – protects a business from employees claiming that their rights are being infringed upon.

- Enterprise coverage – when two or more entities share their resources, such as skills, abilities, personnel, etc.

- Entitlement philosophy – the idea that for each year an employee works, he/she is entitled to a pay raise.

- Environmental disasters – any workplace occurrence that causes harm to the environment, nature, animals, air, land or water.

- Environmental responsibility – an organization's responsibility to the environment, citizens and community in terms of how the business' processes affect health, safety and environment.

- Equipment failure – when machinery or equipment fails to operate properly.

- Equity partnership – a business structure in which individuals or parties invest in a business financially in order to provide start-up capital for a business venture.

- Ergonomics – study of people's efficiency within their work environment.

- Essential job functions – the basic functions of a job.

- Ethics – a set of moral principles. What an individual believes is good and bad in terms of thoughts and actions.

- Evacuations in emergency planning – a written plan as to how an emergency evacuation should be handled and the roles and responsibilities of employees in the event of an evacuation.

- Executive compensation – performance-based rewards for executives or members of management based on how a business performs.

- Executive orders – official documents delivered by the persons in charge of an organization.

- Exit interviews – an interview that is conducted before an employee officially leaves the employ of a business.

- Expatriate – a person living in a country that is not the individual's native land.

- Expense reimbursement – when an individual is paid back for work-related expenses the person initially paid for out of pocket.

- Experience ratings – the value placed on each individual for the amount of experience he/she has acquired.

- External assessment – an organization's outside resources and revenue.

- External business environment – outside factors of a business that impact its performance and the flow of its operations.

F:

- Facilitation for training – how training is administered and who it is administered through.

- Fact-finding in mediation – gathering information by discussing things in a rational way between two or more parties, with a third party to facilitate the discussion.

- Family responsibility discrimination – the right not to be discriminated against as pertains to hiring, employment, promotion or termination because of an individual's responsibility to his/her family.

- Federal document retention requirements – the federal laws that dictate how long a company must keep certain documents.

- Fee-for-service plans – the arrangement that specific services will be provided in return for financial gain.

- Feedback – opinions given by staff members on business practices and principles.

- Fetal protection policies – policies that protect a fetus in the workplace.

- Fiduciary responsibilities – prevalent legal responsibilities by one individual, party, group, organization or business to another.

- Field-review appraisal – when a money lender reviews and appraises specific products in the field, such as in a factory setting.

- Final written warning – the last written warning that an individual or entity receives prior to final actions being taken.

- Financial assets – all assets that can receive a financial valuation and which add additional value to a business.

- First impression bias in interviews – when a business bases its sole opinion on an employment candidate on the first impression that is made rather than taking into consideration the skills, abilities, performance, work history and other assets that that individual can bring to the organization.

- Fiscal year – the financial year, based off accounting purposes, and when taxes are due each year.

- Fitness-for-duty – an individual's physical, emotional and mental competency to do a job effectively and efficiently.

- Flexible spending accounts – an employee puts specific amounts of money into this account that can later be used for the purpose of health-care costs that are out of pocket.

- Flexible work arrangements – a work schedule that allows for flexibility of hours and days of work.

- Focus groups – a diverse group of individuals that provide feedback or input on a product or service.

- Foreign business practices – pertains to all business practices outside the native country that a business is originally from.

- Foreseeable leave – an absence that can be predicted and scheduled.

- Fundamental misrepresentation – when core beliefs, issues or circumstances are misrepresented or misconstrued.

- Functional organization structures – a type of business structure that allows for things to be divided into smaller and more manageable sections.

G:

- Gap analysis – the way in which an organization can recognize its state and compare it to its previous state.

- Garnishment – the legal means by which a debt can be withdrawn from an individual's paycheck prior to the employee receiving payment for time worked.

- Gatekeepers – the individual or employee who controls who has access or is permitted to carry out specific instructions.

- General duties clause – requires the employer to protect employees in cases of serious workplace hazards or dangers.

- General duties standard – the simplest duties required by an individual on the job.

- General partnership – a basic partnership in which two or more parties are invested and reap the rewards, as well as share in any risk.

- Generally accepted accounting principles – the most commonly accepted terms for accounting.

- Geographic marketing – marketing that is based on geographic location.

- Geographic pay – competitive pay based on a person's geographical location in the world rather than an hourly or salary-based pay.

- Global ethics policy – guidelines laid out as a means of avoiding or preventing corruption, bribery and other illegal activities. Companies working internationally often have strict policies for their staff in regard to international work.

- Globalization – a business' mindset to think on a global scale, while still being responsible on a local scale as well.

- Grantor trusts – a trust which belongs to the person who creates it.

- Greenfield operations – when a business builds all new facilities on newly purchased property to start up a new business, facility or plant.

- Grievance – a formal complaint, most often filed through the HR department or through HR personnel, when an employee or member of management is having a serious issue regarding a work issue or conflict.

- Grievance procedure – the process that an organization puts in place in order to address a workplace problem and ensure that the issue is resolved, that all parties involved are treated fairly and that no one party is circumventing the process.

- Gross pay – total money earned before taxes and other deductions.

- Gut-feeling bias in interviews – when ideas and conclusions are made about an individual based on feelings rather than the person's experience, skills, abilities and know-how.

H:

- Halo effect bias in interviews – allowing one area to cloud an interviewer's judgment or opinion.

- Hard bargaining – when compromises are not likely to occur during a negotiation.

- Hardship premium – refers to additional compensation given to an employee placed in a job that is located in an area that results in difficult living conditions.

- Harshness bias in interviews – when a single characteristic is used to evaluate candidates.

- Hazard pay – additional pay that is given to employees in addition to their salary for working in an area that puts their health, physical safety or mental health in immediate or serious peril.

- Headhunting – seeking out employees who work for other companies and offering benefits in addition to salary that might entice these individuals away from their current employers.

- Health and welfare benefits – benefits that are offered for employees' health and welfare such as health insurance, dental insurance, vision insurance, counseling services, sick leave, etc.

- Health and wellness programs – programs that are offered through an employer or health insurance company such as counseling services, gym memberships, etc.

- Hierarchy of needs – a five-tier model of human-based needs, most often shown in the form of a pyramid.

- Hiring management system – a recruiting tool that is implicitly designed to track the recruiting process

- Histograms – diagrams that closely represent a business based on its needs.

- Holiday bonus plans – additional pay that is given as a bonus for being employed with a company at the time of a holiday or for working during a holiday.

- Horn effect bias – cognitive bias.

- Hostile takeovers – when a company is taken over by stockholders who purchase the stocks out from under the owners or replace members of management to gain controlling interest.

- Hostile work environment harassment – when one or more coworkers harass another, creating a tense and uncomfortable work environment. This can include but is not limited to sexual harassment or discrimination.

- Human assets – the abilities, knowledge and skills a person has.

- Human capital and human capital strategies – the ability of a business to employ knowledgeable and talented staff. It also refers to the recruiting methods and compensation a business uses to attract and retain employees.

- HR audits – the evaluation and sorting of HR information and documentation.

- HR information systems – the system used to keep track of employee information for an organization.

- HR outsourcing – the use of an outside source or third party to handle HR tasks for a business.

I:

- I-9 forms – federal form stating that an employee or employment candidate is eligible to work in the United States.

- Immediate vesting – to immediately begin earning a right to carry out a business by working there.

- Implied contracts – when there is not a contract in writing, but the law allows for a contractual obligation to be created in fairness of the parties involved.

- In loco parentis standing – means "in place of the parents" and refers to the legally responsible person.

- Incentives – both financial and non-financial rewards that an employer gives employment candidates or employees in order to incentivize them. This can mean a hiring bonus, increased pay for working the overnight shift, additional PTO time or vacation time, or other similar incentives to convince someone to hire on, stay with a company or move up the career ladder.

- Income statements – a written statement of earnings.

- Independent contractor – individuals that are employed under a contract in which they are paid to do specific tasks. The individuals are not employees of the business but sign a legal contract.

- Indirect compensation – compensation in forms other than money.

- Industrial relations – guidelines, regulations and laws pertaining to relationships between management and staff.

- Information technology – the use of technological systems in businesses in order to become more effective and efficient.

- Initiatives – people's ability to make their own assessment of things and to draw their own conclusions.

- Injunctions – ruling that temporarily stops specific actions from being taken for a period of time.

- Injury and illness compensation program – benefits program that allows compensation such as paid leave, health-care coverage, physical or occupational therapy or other compensation when an employee is hurt on the job or becomes ill.

- Insourcing – when HR uses existing employees or existing departments within an organization to complete tasks, execute work or otherwise complete business. Insourcing is used as an alternative to outsourcing.

- Instructional training methods – a written form of training.

- Insubordination – when an employee goes against orders or does not act in a professional manner.

- Intellectual property – legally recognized ownership of a creation or invention not usually encompassed by the protection of a copyright, patent or trademark.

- Internal conditions and total rewards – a method of planning and making arrangements for the future.

- Internal rate of return – the way that a business measures its profits by averaging the returns for the year or multiple years.

- Internship programs – a program that allows individuals to gain education and work experience through a teaching program in a business. Internships are usually for a given period of time, and that time grants the individual credits for school, a grade or provides other incentives.

- Interpersonal skills – skills that an individual possesses, which allow that individual to communicate and build positive relationships.

- Interventions – to intervene or interrupt in a situation.

- Interviews – a formal meeting where a company representative meets with individuals to examine their skills, abilities, knowledge and work experience in order to ascertain whether they're fit to fill a position within the company.

- Intranet – a private computer network, through the internet that grants limited access to select individuals to the information contained within that network. An example of using an intranet could be a major corporation that has satellite offices around the world. The company information is on an intranet, and only employees that are granted access are able to access that information.

- Intrinsic rewards – psychological rewards such as a sense of accomplishment for work performed.

- Involuntary deductions – deductions taken automatically from an individual's pay, such as taxes or wage garnishments.

- Involuntary exit process – the process by which an employee's services are terminated involuntarily.

- Involvement strategies for employees – the way in which a business motivates employees to get more involved with company matters.

J:

- Job bidding – when businesses compete for a job contract. For example, say a town's city hall needs renovations. Three local construction companies may each bid for the project. This allows the county to choose the most appropriate company for the project.

- Job competencies – the knowledge possessed by an individual, group or business to complete a task or job.

- Job enrichment – motivational techniques that are often used in business to generate a positive and uplifting environment.

- Job evaluation process – a formal analysis, review or other such examination of individuals to decide how well they perform on a given job.

- Job fairs – a gathering of multiple employers that allows employees, the general public and competitors to view the jobs that are available. People can also meet with employers, gather employer information and apply for jobs at such fairs.

- Job postings – an advertisement for a job that is available within an organization.

- Job sharing – when an employee is trained to do more than one job or when multiple employees are hired to share the same job.

- Joint venture – a business partnership in which two or more parties are invested. The risks and rewards of that business venture are then shared by all parties involved. If it fails, both parties fail, but if it succeeds, then all parties involved split the profits.

- Jury duty pay – pay that is given to employees for serving jury duty, rather than working their regular job.

K:

- Key business initiatives – the way in which a business sets its priorities.

- Kidnap and ransom insurance – an insurance policy that protects businesses and employees in the event of a ransom demand. Policies like this are most often purchased by companies that work in high-risk areas worldwide or have owners, staff or associations with high-profile or wealthy members. This insurance protects, pays and reimburses policy holders for losses due to kidnapping and ransom.

- Kinesthetic learners – learning by touch, sight and sound.

L:

- Labor market – jobs that are available in a given area or market.

- Labor relations – the relationship between employees and employers.

- Labor union – employees who come together to seek better wages, benefits, compensation or working conditions from employers.

- Laissez-faire leaders – leaders who do not interfere with matters unless it's absolutely essential.

- Lawful strikes – a refusal to work in order to secure concessions from an employer.

- Layoffs – refers to an employer either temporarily or permanently terminating employees to save money or keep a company going during a difficult time.

- Leadership – the process of influencing the actions of others in order to assist them in accomplishing a common goal.

- Leadership development – when a business invests in its members of management or other leading roles within the organization to help them to be more effective in their current roles or to prepare them for future roles.

- Leapfrogging – to surpass or overtake another.

- Learned professional exemptions – to be exempt or excluded from certain professional educations or qualifications.

- Learning effectiveness model – a business model that ensures that the training and development programs implemented throughout a business are helping the organization meet its immediate and long-term goals.

- Learning management system – a software system that is designed to take some of the workload off HR personnel by tracking the progress of employees' training and continued development. The system provides training materials, tracks individuals' progress as they complete the training material and take tests to ensure their understanding and institutes further development training opportunities. Learning management systems vary from business to business to meet organizations' needs. They can include but are not limited to e-learning, training content, safety protocols, etc.

- Learning portal – an internet-based online pathway that some employers utilize to allows employees to access educational and training resources.

- Leave of absence – time an employee takes off from work, most often for illness or injury or to care for an immediate family member.

- Legal and regulatory activities in business – using the authority of the law to regulate a business' proceedings.

- Legal compliance risk – assuming the financial downfalls of a business and accepting legal responsibilities.

- Licensing – a legal document that shows an individual or organization's right to produce, sell or use a product or service. The product or service is a copyright, intellectual property or trademark owned by the individual or organization, and licensing gives others legal permission to use it as well.

- Leniency bias in interviews – to go easy on someone during an interview because of a particular bias the interviewer has.

- Liabilities – the responsibility assumed by an individual, business or organization in the event that illness or injury should occur from a work-related instance.

- Limited liability company – ownership of a company that renders the owners not personally liable for debts incurred, for which only the business itself can be held liable.

- Limited liability partnership – having two or more members of a partnership sharing the risks and the rewards of a business venture.

- Lobbying – attempting to influence a decision or outcome.

- Lockouts – not allowing employees into a place of business.

- Long-form employment application – a full-length, detailed application.

- Long-range plans – generally at least a five-year plan for a business that puts in writing the plans for future success and how goals will be reached.

- Long-term disability coverage – compensates employees for loss of income due to illness, injury or accident if they are hurt on the job unless a specific policy dictates otherwise.

- Low-context cultures – areas in which information is exceptionally clear-cut and to the point.

- Lump sum compensation – a single payment made for the full amount of money due. This compensation can be for things such as reimbursement for housing or transportation, insurance, travel expenses or other business-related expenses.

M:

- Management – staff members who oversee employees or a business.

- Mandatory benefits – benefits that are required to be provided by employers to their employees by law. Generally, these sorts of benefits are for financial or economic security.

- Marketing functions – a process that assists companies in determining if a product will be successful, the marketplace that it is most likely to sell in and the clientele that is most likely to purchase such a product. Some of this research is gathered by making comparisons to similar products already on the market.

- Marketplace – the physical and virtual places that businesses operate. Today, the global marketplace is often a virtual platform.

- Market salary survey – research that is conducted by a business in order to determine what the average pay for any given job on the market is. This is done as a way for organizations to stay competitive and fair when offering a salary for a given job.

- Mass layoffs – when large numbers of employees are either temporarily or permanently let go from their jobs.

- Material safety data sheet – an OSHA-regulated and required document for workplace hazards.

- Meal periods compensation – a federal law that does not require breaks but does not prevent meal periods that can be taken by employees while on duty.

- Mediation – when a dispute occurs and another party is brought in to help work through the situation.

- Mentoring – when a business uses experienced personnel to help new employees by sharing their experience and knowledge.

- Merger – when two or more organizations join together in a business venture and become a new, shared, legal entity. A merger occurs when the organizations involved purchase one or the other or legally share their joint resources. Mergers generally happen as a means of saving money, streamlining business structures and making businesses more efficient.

- Merit increase – refers to when a business gives pay raises to employees for reaching job performance goals.

- Minimum wage – the legal minimum a business can pay an employee for doing a job.

- Mission statement – a description of a business' stated purpose. This purpose is not something that changes, but rather stays constant within that organization.

- Mitigation of risks – limiting the likelihood of risk in a given situation.

- Mobility – a term used by HR to label employees who relocate for work.

- Mobility premium – a bonus or an additional amount to an employee's salary, paid to an employee for working in another country.

- Monetary compensation – financial compensation paid to an employee in exchange for labor.

- Moonlighting – a term that refers to an individual who works for multiple companies at the same time.

- Moral absolutes – a clearly defined idea of what is right and what is wrong.

N:

- Narrative appraisal methods – an in-depth appraisal that is conducted and often used for legal recourse later on.

- Negative emphasis bias in interviews – when negative feedback is used to make hiring decisions.

- Negligent hiring – legal claim that an employer is responsible for hiring employees without vetting them beforehand.

- Negotiating – bargaining to ensure that people involved get some or all of what is being discussed.

- Neutrality agreements – an agreement made between a union and an employee in which an employee agrees to support the union in regard to any actions taken against the employer.

- No strike/no lockout clause – employees who have this employment clause cannot strike or partake in a lockout. Doing so would invalidate their contract and could lead to their immediate dismissal.

- Noise exposure standard – the safe standard at which people can be exposed to noise or need protection to prevent hearing damage.

- Nonbinding arbitration – when parties use a third party to help them settle a legal disagreement. However, if the agreement displeases one or both parties, the final call of the arbitration does not have to stand, and the outcome may be challenged.

- Nondirective interviews – interviews that are done in a way that answers are taken as they are presented, and there is no attempt to interpret responses.

- Nondisclosure agreement – a legally binding agreement that ensures that all parties agree not to share specific confidential information.

- Nonessential job functions – job functions that do not qualify as part of the core job though they may fall under its general umbrella.

- Nonmonetary compensation – compensation that is not financial, such as health benefits, gym memberships, club invitations and more.

- Nonqualified retirement plans – retirement plans that do not follow the Employment Retirement Income Security Administration guidelines.

- Nontraditional pay structures – a way of paying employees that is not typical.

O:

- Objectives – goals a business sets.

- Offer letters – an official written job offer.
- Offshoring – when a business moves to another country because labor, supplies or operations are cheaper.
- Ombudsman – an individual who has been officially appointed to verify the validity of a complaint and is a mandated public reporter in the event that the complaint is substantiated.
- On-call workers – on-call employees must be available to work when called upon. They may be required to live near the workplace.
- On-the-job experience – the knowledge and skills employees gain as they perform day-to-day duties.
- Open-door policy – a policy that allows employees to communicate directly with upper management in the event that an issue arises.
- Organizational development – a process used by businesses to assist them in planning, implementing and organizing the workplace.
- Orientation programs – provides new employees with information about their employer and their new place of employment. Can also include initial training programs.
- Outplacement – assistance to employees that have been laid off in order to help those people find jobs elsewhere.
- Outsourcing – when a business hires a third party to do some work.

- Overtime – time paid after an individual's typical eight-hour shift or anything over the initial 40-hour week. This time is rewarded with time and a half pay.

P:

- Paid time off – time that is earned by an employee for hours worked, and that can later be used in order to take paid time off.

- Paired comparison appraisal method – a decision-making tool used for setting and comparing values.

- Panel interview – an interview in which an employment candidate goes before three or more members of HR or management as part of the interview process.

- Parallel bargaining – when a union negotiates for benefits, compensation and wages that are fairly similar to agreements previously made.

- Parental leave – a specific period of time, usually twelve to thirteen weeks, that a parent can take off from work to look after a child. This time is most often not paid and is usually taken by a father since mothers are afforded maternity leave.

- Partnerships – partners that share in the risk and reward of a business venture.

- Passive training method – a way of training in which an instructor conveys information to students.

- Patents – legal document that shows proof of ownership and limits the production, use and sale of a product to the patent owner.

- Path-goal theory of leadership – refers to leadership styles, goal achievements, employee motivations and overall employee productivity.

- Patterned interviews – this type of interview is most commonly used when hiring personnel for areas of work, including education and work history, but allows for an open dialogue and questions with defined points.

- Pay differentials – the difference between a person's skills and a job's wages.

- Pay equity – the principle that equal work value merits equal pay.

- Pay ranges – the boundaries that the pay for a given position can range from.

- Payroll – the process of calculating individuals' hours and pay per hour, completing timesheets, cutting checks and distributing checks.

- Performance appraisal – the regular review of employees' job performance.

- Performance-based compensation – compensation received by employees that is in direct correlation with the work that they are doing, the level of performance that they are achieving and the amount of time they are dedicating to their jobs.

- Performance management programs – set performance expectations for a given job. Management is responsible for enforcing these expectations, and individuals are expected to be accountable to themselves and ensure that they are meeting their self-established goals and milestones.

- Permanent arbitrators – these individuals serve as arbitrators for the entire life of a given contract. This usually occurs through a mutual agreement of all parties involved.

- Personal protective equipment – equipment that is used to protect an individual. Such equipment can include face coverings or masks, rubberized boots, hazmat suits, gloves, rubberized gloves, face shields, goggles, safety glasses and hardhats. Other equipment such as respirators, oxygen tanks and anything else that can be used to protect an individual's eyes, mouth, nose, airway, head and skin is also personal protective equipment.

- Personnel functions – motivation and management of staff, and assisting with training and development.

- Phantom stock – also known as shadow stocks, these are offered to management without legally transferring ownership of stock to those individuals.

- Physical assets – assets like this can include inventory, office supplies, office furniture, machinery and other items that are intangible. Physical assets can also include buildings, land, outbuildings and shops.

- Physical job requirements – the physical requirements that are demanded of a position, such as bending, twisting, standing for long periods of time, sitting for long periods of time and other things that need to be done bodily in order to meet the qualifications for the job.

- Picketing – employees who are picketing refuse to work as they negotiate working conditions, wages or any other matters intended to improve their work environment.

- Plant closing – when an entire facility closes, most or all of its employees are laid off, machinery and any other items of value are sold or repurposed at another facility and any employees who are not laid off are transferred to a different location.

- Plant patents – intellectual property that is protected by the facility in which it was developed and produced.

- Point of service plans – a health-care plan that offers different coverage for in-network and out-of-network services.

- Policies – the procedures that are put in place for employees to follow to ensure the efficient running of a business.

- Position summary – a detailed outline of what a job entails, including the skills the ideal candidate needs to possess in order to effectively do the job, as well as the job's responsibilities.

- Positive employee relations strategies – the principle of building good bonds between employees and management in order to facilitate positive relationships, encourage honest feedback from employees and generate a healthy environment.

- Practice analysis study – a study in which information is gathered to determine the specific skills required for a particular job.

- Pre-employment tests – testing that is done prior to employment to ensure that employment candidates possess the skills for the position that they are applying for. Additionally, testing may be done regarding an individual's personality or ability to handle stress depending on the job's expectations.

- Preliminary order of reinstatement – being reinstated to a job pending further review.

- Prescription coverage – health insurance coverage that includes prescription medications that employees and their families may need.

- Principle bargaining – effectively negotiating for fair, market-valued, law-abiding, high-standard and industrially efficient principles and protocol.

- Product and operations functions – increasing production and efficiency, streamlining processes and consistently improving customer service.

- Professional development – opportunities for employees to receive ongoing education and training so as to improve their skills and knowledge.

- Professional responsibilities – these include being accountable, respecting confidentiality, being fiscally responsible, honest, and having integrity, following the law, being objective and working transparently.

- Profit and loss statements – a financial statement that shows all of the earnings that a business has earned over a period of time, the costs and expenses that have occurred and how much profit has been lost.

- Profit-sharing plans – when a business divides up the profits and shares a percentage with others.

- Project management concepts – the initiating, planning, conducting, monitoring and conclusion of a project. This can include integration, work scope, time, cost, quality, HR, communications, risk management, etc. Ultimately it is all of the moving parts that make up a project.

- Promissory estoppel – when verbal promises are made and then are legally enforced later on.

- Promotion – when employees move up the career ladder or move up within the business that employs them. This advancement requires the employees to take on more responsibility, often for an increase in salary, and sometimes includes a heavier workload.

- Proprietary – information, developmental methods or physical materials that are developed and owned by an organization.

- Publicity picketing – a picket or march preventing employees from working as a form of protest against business practices.

Q:

- Qualifications – the skills, abilities and knowledge that a potential employment candidate or employee has.

- Qualified deferred compensation plans – a legal order that allows compensation to be delayed or deferred.

- Qualified domestic relations orders – a legal order that splits a retirement plan.

- Qualified stock options – stock options that are only offered to the employees of the company.

- Question guidelines for interviews – an outline of questions and protocol that should be followed in order to offer the most fair and comprehensive interview to each employment candidate.

- Question inconsistency bias in interviews – asking different questions to different candidates in a way that results in vastly different answers for candidates seeking the same position of employment.

- Quid pro quo – a favor or advantage given to an employee in return for an employer giving the employee something. This scenario may be reversed as well.

R:

- Raise – an increase in an employee's salary due to job performance, time on the job, annual reviews or seniority.

- Random drug testing – the randomized testing of employees for drugs, alcohol or other illicit substances while on the job.

- Range placement for pay structure – employees' pay based off a scale range that is dependent on their placement.

- Reasonable accommodations – accommodations made by an employer in order for an individual with a disability to be able to do a job effectively.

- Reasonable expectation of privacy – the expectation by employees that they will receive a certain level of privacy while in the workplace, on work property or while conducting business for their employer.

- Recognitional picketing – when employees picket in order to gain recognition and seek to have their employer negotiate with them.

- Record retention schedule – the specific amount of time that the HR department or other departments within a business are required to keep documents and hard copies of information. Those documents are kept for either legal reasons or because of company policies. Once the time frame for keeping these documents has been exceeded, only then can those documents or that information be deleted or destroyed.

- Recovery of back wages – a method of being paid what an employee is owed in terms of past-due wages and compensation.

- Recruitment – the process of attracting qualified individuals to apply for job openings within an organization.

- Red flag – a term that refers to warning signs on an application, in a person's behavior or which otherwise suggest that an individual may not be the right fit for a job.

- Reference check – the process of confirming employment with an individual's past employers and calling references to get their feedback on an individual.

- Regulatory activities – reasonable and necessary actions needed to maintain approval, stay within regulations or otherwise conduct a clinical trial.

- Reimbursement – the act of paying back an individual, group, entity, business or organization for money that was paid upfront for work-related expenses.

- Relocation services – when a business hires movers to help pack up an employee and move the person to a new location for work. This can also include things such as connecting that employee with a realtor to help the person rent or purchase a home in the new location, pay for travel expenses, cover the cost of taxes or otherwise pay for costs associated with relocating.

- Repatriation – an employee's move back home after working abroad.
- Reporting premiums – a list of assets covered, claims paid or other such information when an insurance policy is up for renewal.
- Research and development functions – provisions to make improvements and develop an organization.
- Resignations – a formal written notice that a person is leaving a position with a business.
- Rest period compensation – federally regulated periods of rest that are required to ensure the health and safety of employees.
- Restricted stock – specific constraints placed on an employee that limit the time frame in which they can sell or offload stocks.
- Restructuring – reworking the way in which an organization is structured or operates.
- Retention bonuses – an additional sum paid to employees for staying with a business.
- Retention programs – programs that help businesses keep existing employees.
- Return on investment – the evaluation of an investment. This is measured in the same way in which the financial outcome of a business is measured.

- Return-to-work programs – programs that allow employees to return to work at a limited or reduced capacity while they are still ill or recovering.

- Reverse discrimination – the practice of favoring a specific group that is typically discriminated against.

- Risk management – the process of assessing threats and possible hazards within a business and working to limit or eliminate them.

S:

- Sabbatical leave – when an employee is given a specific amount of time off from work, with pay, to study, rest or travel.

- Safe harbor provisions – legal arrangements that help to lower, stop or at least regulate situations in order to lessen the chances of a hostile takeover.

- Safety training programs – programs that are specifically designed to teach safe work practices.

- Sales and marketing function – functions that generate revenue within a business.

- Sales bonuses – a bonus or additional compensation given to employees who reach a given sales quota.

- Screening interviews – part of the interview process where job candidates are assessed to see whether they meet the basic qualifications in order to advance any further in the interviewing process.

- Screening tools – a way of assessing employees to decide if they are suited for specific positions within a business.

- Seasonal workers – employees who work for a specific season or holiday.
- Self-assessment – when employees are given the opportunity to reflect on their own performance.
- Self-directed work teams – a group of employees who take responsibility for managing themselves and ensuring that they stay on task without a supervisor micromanaging or controlling the workflow.
- Self-funded insurance plans – an insurance plan in which the employer pays for most or all of the benefits' costs.
- Self-paced training – training that can be done at whatever pace the employee feels is effective.
- Seniority-based compensation systems – compensation awarded to employees based on the number of years served in an organization.
- Severance – a payment made to employees when they are laid off or fired.
- Sexual harassment – unwelcome behavior that is seen to be offensive in a verbal, visual or sexual manner.
- Shareholders – individuals that own shares in a business or corporation.
- Shift pay – pay that varies based on whether the employee works first shift, second shift or third shift.

- Short-form applications – an application that can be completed on a smartphone or tablet.

- Short-term disability insurance – insurance that provides wage compensation, health benefits and other possible benefits for when an employee is ill and has to take a short period of time off work to recuperate.

- Sick pay – pay that is earned from the number of hours an employee works and which can later be used in order to pay for time that an employee has to take off from work due to an illness.

- Simulation models – the process of creating different models and testing them out to determine which model has the most practical real-world application

- Sit-down strikes – a strike that takes place in the place of employment and prevents others from taking the strikers' place while the strike is ongoing

- Skills training – expressly designed to give employees training that is focused on the skills, abilities and knowledge that they need. It can be used as an initial education tool, a continuing education tool or a re-education tool.

- Skip-level interviews – one-on-one interviews or meetings that take place between employees and management.

- S.M.A.R.T Goal Setting – S.M.A.R.T. stands for Specific, Measurable, Action-Oriented, Realistic and Time-Based. This goal-setting method is designed to assist businesses and organizations in reaching their goals.

- Social concerns – issues that deal with the interaction between people.

- Social networking – social interactions that are communicated for the purpose of shared interests. In terms of business, this can be a key point of contact for advertising, business expansion and much more.

- Sole proprietorships – a business that is not separate from the business owner. Income and taxes are all included with the business owner's personal taxes.

- Sourcing and recruiting – identifying and drawing qualified employment applicants for open positions within a business.

- Span of control – the number of subordinates or employees under a manager's direct supervision or control.

- Split payroll – for employees working internationally, this can be when part of an individual's salary is paid in two currencies. The first currency is the currency of the country where the person is working, and the second currency is that of the person's country of origin.

- Staffing needs analysis – the evaluation and compilation of data that helps to determine the future staffing needs of a business.

- Stakeholder – an individual, group, business or organization that has an interest in an organization. This interest can be either direct or indirect. Stakeholders can include but are not limited to owners, employees, investors or suppliers.

- Start-up – a new business venture. This term is more specifically used during the development, initial investments and early operations phases of a business' inception.

- State unemployment insurance – state tax-funded protection for employees to receive unemployment insurance for a short period of time if they lose their jobs.

- Statements of cash flow – financial statement of a business' revenue and expenses.

- Statutory deductions – deductions that are required by law. An employer has no choice but to withhold these deductions as a matter of law.

- Stereotyping bias in interviewers – making assumptions or drawing conclusions about individuals based on their looks or the way they sound before taking the time to complete an interview.

- Stock options – the opportunity or option to purchase stocks within a business. It's not uncommon to offer stocks to employees as part of their benefits and compensation options.

- Stockholders – shareholders that own part of a company.

- Stop-loss insurance – protections that are provided in the event of an incredible loss for a business.

- Straight-line operations – a way of operating in which one thing flows smoothly into the next.

- Strategic interventions – a program designed to facilitate planning, strategy and skills in order to change things up.

- Strategic management areas – when the four priority areas of an organization are brought together for the benefit of a company as a whole, including marketing, operations, finance and HR.

- Strategic partnership program – when businesses join together for their mutual benefit.

- Strategic workforce planning – the process by which an organization anticipates the hiring needs that it currently has and the future hiring needs it will have.

- Stress interviews – an interview technique that is used to put candidates under high levels of stress in order to see how they handle themselves under pressure.

- Strikes – when work or operations are stopped and employees refuse to continue their work as a means of voicing their discontent for a situation, mistreatment or grievance.

- Structured interviews – interviews that have a clear outline that is followed by the interviewer.

- Subcontractor – an individual, group, business or organization that completes smaller tasks or jobs for another entity on a larger project.

- Succession planning – a carefully drafted outline of how leadership roles in a business will shift in the event that members of management retire, step down, pass away or are otherwise removed from their leadership roles.

- Summary plan descriptions – a written plan that outlines the inner workings of a given entity or process.

- Supervisor assessments – the reviewing of employees' work and roles.

- Supervisory responsibilities – the responsibility of a supervisor or member of management to oversee, manage and otherwise assist employees.

- Supervisory training – when a supervisor or member of management handles the training of personnel or employees.

- Sustainability – a business' ability to start and maintain a business venture.

T:

- Tactical accountability measures – having members of management hold the appropriate individuals accountable for certain business measures.

- Talent assessment – method of finding the appropriate candidates for the right positions within a business.

- Talent management – the attraction, acquiring, developing, motivating and retaining of talented, high-performance employees.

- Target benefits plans – an estimated monthly benefits plan that is adjustable and which can change from month to month.

- Task force – a small group or team that is brought together in order to complete a project.

- Tax equalization policy – a policy for international employees that arranges for taxes to be paid in the country the individuals are working in, as well as the countries they are residents of. Ideally, employees do not pay a higher tax than what they would have paid in their countries of origin alone.

- Team-building activities – activities that allow members of a team that work together to do non-work-related activities as a means of strengthening their communication skills. Team-building activities can include things such as bowling, roller skating, paintball, etc.

- Technological factors – advancements and changes in technology that allow a business to become more efficient based on the technology the organization has access to.

- Telecommunications – refers to the process of working from home while using a computer.

- Temporary workers – refers to employees who are hired to work for a short duration, at the end of which their employment is terminated.

- Termination – when employees quit their position or are fired.

- Termination clauses – the agreed-upon terms by which employees may quit their job or by which an employer may sever a person's employment.

- Terms and conditions of employment – the outlined agreement of an individual's employment terms, including job responsibilities and agreed-upon compensation.

- Tenure – a permanent job within a business that has renewals at set intervals. It is exceedingly difficult to remove an employee from a tenured contract.

- 360-degree feedback – a process used in the HR department in order to collect internal and external information about a business and its employees to determine key information about the organization. This feedback is gathered from all employment levels, including upper management, lower management, suppliers and customers.

- Third-party contract management – when an organization hires an outside party to manage the business' contracts.

- Time-off programs – an arrangement allows employees to schedule a set amount of paid time off. This time can be used for vacation, personal time, sick leave, etc.

- Time-series forecasts – uses a business' past valuations in order to predict future revenue.

- Time to fill – the typical amount of time that it takes for a business to find a qualified applicant to fill a vacant position.

- Timing for performance appraisals – the regular review of employees' performance in their current positions within a business.

- Top-down budgeting – when senior managers compile a high-level budget for the company that they are working for.

- Torts – wrongful acts that have civil liabilities.

- Total compensation – base salary and any additional compensation that employees receive for the work that they are doing.

- Total quality management – management style that focuses on maintaining high standards and work principles.

- Town hall meeting – a meeting held for political or business purposes in order to answer questions and give information.

- Training – teaching an employee how things operate in a job, task or organization.

- Transactional leadership – a former of leadership that values the structure of an organization.

- Travel-time compensation – when an employer pays for an employee's travel time. For example, this may be the time it takes an employee to drive from the office to the restaurant where the employee is having dinner with business clients.

- Turnover analysis – the collection of information to determine the rate at which a business experiences turnover and what the cause of such turnover is.

- Tuition reimbursement – a benefit that is offered by some employers to pay for part or all of an employee's school tuition. This is most often done as a condition of working for an organization for an extended period of time.

- Turnkey operation – a business that is purchased and is ready to operate. It includes everything needed to start business upon finalizing the sale.

- Two-factor theory – the idea that there are certain things that can cause satisfaction or dissatisfaction within a workplace.

U:

- Undue hardship provision – actions that an employer may choose to take in order to assist employees through hard times.

- Unemployment insurance – insurance that assists employees in the event that their positions are temporarily or permanently terminated. This gives those employees affected temporarily continued wages while they wait for reinstatement of their employment or seek alternative employment.

- Unexpected loss of key employees – when vital employees leave their employ, with little or no notice.

- Unfair labor practices – unfair treatment of employees.

- Unions – an organization that is designed to work for the best interests of the employees.

- Upfront costs – the money that has to be initially invested in a business to get it started. It can also be the money required in order to finalize the sale of a business.

- Unlawful strikes – strikes whose purpose or cause are illegal.

- Use of confidential information – the use of information that is private to a person, group, organization, business or entity.

- Utility patents – patents that pertain to new creations, improved creations or useful inventions.

V:

- Vacation pay – paid time that is generally accrued for time worked or a set number of paid hours given to employees for the time they have spent with a company.

- Values and ethics in organizations – what a company or organization regards as valuable or of importance.

- Variable compensation – multiple methods, such as a salary and benefits, used as compensation for employees' work.

- Vendor selection – when a business chooses the most beneficial vendors or third-party providers to assist the business in receiving needed supplies.

- Verbal warnings – when an individual, group or entity commits a wrongdoing and is verbally reprimanded.

- Vicarious liabilities – when one individual, group, or entity is held in part responsible for the actions of another party. Such responsibilities most often occur when the other party has done something illegal.

- Virtual work teams – teams that work together in the employment environment towards a common goal or on a common project as a means of helping everyone involved to complete the task successfully.

- Voluntary arbitration – when a dispute arises and the various parties involved choose to have a third party assist in the resolution of the dispute.

- Voluntary deductions – money that employees choose to have withheld from their pay. This can be additional taxes, additional funds added to a pension or retirement plan or other similar withholdings.

W:

- Wage band – the span from the lowest salary that a business will pay an employee to the highest salary.

- Wage compensation – the financial compensation that employees receive for the work that they put in.

- Wages – fixed pay that an employee receives on a regular basis.

- Walk-in candidates – someone that comes into a facility in order to apply for a job rather than applying online or by alternative means.

- Warnings for disciplinary actions – a formal document notifying an employing that he/she will receive disciplinary action.

- Weighted averages – allows for the numerical evaluation of employees to be compiled into comparable data.

- Weighted employment applications – when the responses found on an application or work form are given a numerical value. Those values are used in order to measure the candidate or employee against others.

- Wellness benefits – benefits afforded in an effort to improve the health, wellness or fitness of employees in the workplace. These may be provided directly by the employer or through an insurance program.

- Whistleblower protection – protects those who report others for illegal, unethical or otherwise harmful actions in the workplace.

- Word-of-mouth communications – refers to the dialogue used on a daily basis within a business.

- Work environment – the environment in which employees work or operate. This may include environments such as an office, plant, shop or factory.

- Workforce expansion – when a business expands by adding employees or positions, increasing production or sales and working to generate revenue.

- Workforce planning – the task of looking at a business' current composition, assessing long-term goals and making a plan as to what needs to be done to reach these. This includes looking at the size of the organization now and where it's headed, the type of business it is and the demand and competition for such an entity.

- Workforce reduction – the downsizing of a business. This may include but is not limited to layoffs, reorganization or restructuring of the workplace.

- Work/life benefits – nontraditional benefits offered to employees in order to help them attain a work-life balance in their career.

- Work/life discrimination – occurs when employees are overlooked or dismissed from opportunities of advancement because they have commitments to take care of outside of work, and employees who have no outside commitments are given preference.

- Wrongful termination – occurs when the employer fires or terminates the employee by violating or breaking the terms of the employment contract.

Y:

- Yellow-dog contracts – contracts that are made between an employer and employees wherein employees agree not to partake in a union of any kind for the duration of their employment.

Z:

- Zero-based budgeting – a budget method that requires expenses to be justified for each fiscal period.

Human Resources Ethical Codes

Human resources professionals are responsible for maintaining a high standard of professional ethics. Every HR employee is responsible for:

- Increasing the value of an organization
- Building and maintaining professional and ethical practices within an organization
- Working within the constraints of local, state and federal laws
- Increasing the performance and services of the HR department and the organization as a whole
- Ensuring the social responsibility and performance responsibilities of the HR department and the organization as a whole
- Advocating for employees
- Being open to input in regard to decision making and the outcome of those decisions and how they affect staff
- Ensuring quality training, continued education and opportunities for skills development for HR personnel, employees, etc.

- Ensuring ethical behavior and responsibility throughout all professional interactions and business dealings
- Ensuring respect for every individual
- Following business policies
- Following conflict resolution policies
- Ensuring that a person's position in HR is never abused for personal gain
- Ensuring that HR reps meet the obligations of a position and disclose conflicts appropriately to stakeholders.
- Avoiding special treatment of other individuals
- Properly and ethically managing sensitive information

Human Resources as a Department and HR Personnel Job Requirements

As a member of the HR department, your job will entail three key functions: administrative duties, operations duties and strategizing for the business.

Administrative Duties

The administrative duties that are the responsibility of HR personnel include:

- Keeping detailed records on all of the information that HR has access to
- Maintaining records in regard to job databases within the organization
- Tracking and retaining information and documentation as it relates to advertising, recruiting, applications, interviews, hiring, orientation, training, professional development, promotions, retirement and termination
- Keeping detailed records and files regarding employees (past and present), including new-hire paperwork, information on employee salaries and raises, performance evaluations and annual reviews and termination forms for employees who have been fired or resigned
- Posting job listings for vacant positions or when a new position is created

- Interviewing employment candidates, eliminating those who are underqualified or who do not otherwise seem to be a good fit for the position and moving qualified candidates through the interviewing process
- Arranging hiring offers, negotiating new-hire terms and processing all new-hire documents
- Arranging and administering orientation, training and professional career development
- Ensuring that all required I-9 forms and immigration-related procedures and

  paperwork are handled appropriately.
- Maintaining all payroll-related information.
- Providing workers' compensation forms to staff as appropriate and taking care of all workers' compensation, short-term disability and long-term disability claims as dictated by company policy.

Operational Duties

The operational duties that are the responsibility of HR personnel include:

- Ensuring compliance with all applicable local, state and federal laws
- Working with other HR personnel in regard to recruitment, COBRA insurance, employment services, etc.
- Providing customer service, support services and information as it relates to employees and HR
- Providing adequate and appropriate information regarding workplace policies and procedures
- Identifying risks within the workplace
- Maintaining a list of jobs within the organization, ensuring that job functions and duties are updated regularly and supporting managers in this capacity
- Screening job applicants (and, in some cases, doing initial interviews) for members of management including team leaders and department managers
- Answering job and hiring-related questions

- Conducting interviews
- Informing individuals about benefits and compensation programs offered, including employees' health and wellness plans and retirement or pension planning
- Making arrangements for the orientation of new employees or transferred employees
- Conducting performance reviews for employees.

Strategizing Duties

The strategizing duties that are the responsibility of HR personnel include supporting, communicating and implementing the company culture, ethics, mission, values and vision.

I. Company culture refers to the beliefs held by an organization such as company expectations, rules, processes and procedures. Company culture is a company's worldview and the idea of what impact the business wants to have as an organization.

II. A mission statement is a brief, detailed description regarding the purposes and goals of the company. A mission statement is unchanged for the life of most businesses.

III. A vision statement is a written statement that makes clear where the business wants to go, and what the future of the company holds.

IV. Values of a business refer to what the company as a whole perceives as good and desirable and what isn't.

Running a Business and the Role of Human Resources

Human resources personnel must be able to implement business principles and practices. Understanding how to effectively implement changes in a business is part of an ever-evolving HR department.

While a small business such as a sole proprietorship or partnership can be handled by the owner or partners, larger entities such as limited liability companies, corporations and franchises are more likely to need an HR department in order to manage the bulk of company affairs.

There are three documents that are most important for managing the financial aspects of a business: balance sheets, income statements and statements of cash flow.

A balance sheet is a simple visual representation of what a company has in assets, liabilities and equity. It is important for a business to have that information ready, to ensure it is prepared when making decisions regarding hiring and firing, sales and purchases and acquisitions and mergers.

Income statements are a quick look at what a business currently has in sales, expenses and net income. Income statements show the total in an organization's sales. The expense of running the business is deducted from the money earned in sales in order to calculate net income. Knowing its net income is vital for a business. Therefore, this is an important document for HR personnel to keep track of.

Finally, it is important that HR personnel track a business' cash flow. A cash-flow statement shows the physical money that a business has, such as in a bank account. The statement shows how much money a business has that is not wrapped up in products, services, operation costs or staffing. A business should know whether it has a positive or negative cash flow at all times. Maintaining an up-to-date cash-flow statement is part of daily HR responsibilities.

When it comes to HR maintaining an organization's budget, there are two commonly used budgeting methods—incremental and zero-based. An incremental budget is built over a fiscal year. Such budgets depend on the goals of the business, the objectives on how to reach those goals, the needs of personnel, the expenses that will be incurred by adding equipment or services to a business and any additional singular costs that may crop up along the way.

Zero-based budgets, on the other hand, start at zero at the beginning of each fiscal year. With these budgets, HR can see a direct correlation between the money that is earned or generated and expenses that will come out of those earnings as they rise. HR must review either type of budget and determine what the business has in terms of budgets for new employees, benefits packages, compensation, merit bonuses, raises and other similar financial expenditures that may be made in regards to employee relations.

HR must also focus on returns on investments, research and development, marketing and sales, operations in operation costs and information technology. These items can simplify and streamline the employment process.

- A return on investment (ROI) is a calculation done to determine the outcome of an investment. It takes into account when an investment begins earning money, pays back the initial investment that was made and begins to generate revenue.

- Developing new ideas or improving existing ones is particularly important for a business. When HR facilitates the hiring of new employees, it's important to look for candidates who not only have the qualifications for the job but who also bring fresh eyes and insight to it as well.

- Advertising and sales generate money for a business. The money earned off a product, service or idea is all profit after the production costs are deducted.

- A business' information technology (IT) can help it succeed. IT can include hardware, software, databases, e-commerce, e-learning and more. It can make the job of HR personnel much easier by tracking and totaling employee timecards, streamlining payroll services and helping to make orders and shipments more organized while requiring fewer people to be involved.

Test 1 (100 Questions)

Read each of the following questions carefully. Then choose the best answer for each question.

1. As an HR professional, understanding and managing a business' inner workings and employees is an example of:

    (A) Management

    (B) Operations

    (C) Mediation

    (D) Performance

2. The individuals or groups that generate revenue for a business are known as:

    (A) Staff units

    (B) Team leaders

    (C) Line management

    (D) Focus groups

3. When behavioral science is utilized as a means of improving how a business functions, this is as known as:

    (A) Organizational development

    (B) Distributive technique

    (C) Compensatory training

    (D) Delphine technique

4. A full HR department is not necessary in:

(A) A large corporation

(B) An industrial production plant

(C) A small business

(D) A franchise

5. The Occupational Safety and Health Administration was created :

(A) To audit high-profile organizations

(B) For employee health and safety

(C) To protect employees from harassment

(D) To put checks and balances in place

6. The process of recruiting employees to a business includes all of the following except:

(A) Advertising

(B) Training

(C) Interviewing

(D) Screening

7. Reviewing employment applications, meeting with potential employment candidates, eliminating employment candidates who do not meet the key qualifications for the position that needs to be filled, and arriving at the candidates who could best fill a position is an example of:

(A) The interview process

(B) The coaching process

(C) The promotion process

(D) The layoff process

8. An organization's size and the number of employees will determine:

(A) The wages of each employee

(B) The amount of time required to interview employees

(C) The number of breaks an employee is entitled to

(D) The size of the HR department required

9. Which of the following correctly states the purpose of OSHA within a business?

(A) OSHA is responsible for ensuring that companies are paying their employees at least minimum wage and providing basic health care as required by law.

(B) OSHA is responsible for making sure that companies are meeting EPA standards and leaving small carbon footprints whenever possible.

(C) OSHA is responsible for ensuring the overall health and safety of employees.

(D) OSHA is responsible for cleaning up chemical waste that is spilled or otherwise impacting the environment.

10. Which of the following is a resource that businesses can utilize in order to attract qualified individuals for potential employment?

(A) Promotions

(B) Advertisements

(C) Severance packages

(D) Development programs

11. Once an employee is hired, the employee will go through which of the following steps in order to ensure they are well prepared to fulfill the job requirements?

    (A) Orientation

    (B) Training

    (C) Continued education

    (D) All of the above

12. Under which law are employers required to make reasonable accommodations for any employees with disabilities to allow such individuals to perform their jobs?

    (A) Americans with Disabilities Act

    (B) Genetic Information Nondiscrimination Act

    (C) Uniformed Services Employment and Reemployment Rights Act

    (D) Occupational Safety and Health Act

13. Individuals under which age are not covered by the Age Discrimination in Employment Act?

    (A) 18

    (B) 30

    (C) 60

    (D) 40

14. Under which of the following laws are employees required to be given the choice to keep their health insurance coverage if they are affected by temporary layoffs, job loss, reduction in hours, changes in position of employment, the death of an immediate family member, or a disruption in their typical life events?

    (A) The Consolidated Omnibus Budget Reconciliation Act

    (B) The Occupational Safety and Health Act

    (C) The Americans with Disabilities Act

    (D) The Family and Medical Leave Act

15. When employees take advantage of the privileges afforded to them under the Consolidated Omnibus Budget Reconciliation Act, they are required to:

    (A) File for unemployment insurance

    (B) Pay into a 401k plan

    (C) Pay their typical insurance premiums

    (D) Accept their pension

16. The Shareholder Disclosure, Approval of golden parachutes, Say-on-Pay, and Say-on-Pay frequency are all covered under:

    (A) The Occupational Safety and Hazard Act

    (B) The Employee Retirement Income Security Act

    (C) The Fair Credit Reporting Act

    (D) The Wall Street Reform and Consumer Protection Act

17. The Employee Retirement Income Security Act is administered, supervised, and enforced by:

   (A) The Department of Homeland Security

   (B) The Civil Liberties Commission

   (C) The Department of Labor

   (D) The Senior Citizens' Representation and Protection Board

18. The Family and Medical Leave Act is known by:

   (A) FMLA

   (B) OSHA

   (C) FCRA

   (D) FBSA

19. Which of the following acts sets the standard minimum wage?

   (A) The Equal Pay Act

   (B) The Civil Rights Act

   (C) The Fair Credit Reporting Act

   (D) The Fair Labor Standards Act

20. Which of the following laws prevents health insurance companies from denying coverage to individuals or charging higher premiums due to a genetic predisposition to a health issue but not an illness that a person actually has at the time coverage is sought?

   (A) The Family and Medical Leave Act

   (B) The Health Insurance Portability and Accountability Act

   (C) The Genetic Information Nondiscrimination Act

   (D) The Fair Labor Standards Act

21. Which of the following acronyms is the more commonly used label for the Health Insurance Portability and Accountability Act?

(A) FMLA

(B) FLSA

(C) NLRA

(D) HIPAA

22. Which of the following forms is the federal document that is required to be completed by job applicants or employees in regard to immigration status, naturalization, and an individual's right to work in the United States?

(A) W-2

(B) I-9

(C) W-4

(D) 1099

23. Which of the following organizations is responsible for implementing and enforcing OSHA regulations?

(A) The Department of Labor

(B) The Civil Liberties Commission

(C) The Equal Employment Opportunities Commission

(D) The Department of Health and Human Services

24. Obamacare was formally known as:

(A) The Family and Medical Leave Act

(B) The Patient Protection and Affordable Care Act

(C) The Health Insurance Portability and Accountability Act

(D) The Genetic Information Nondiscrimination Act

25. Failure by any individual to purchase health insurance coverage under the Patient Protection and Affordable Care Act used to result in:

(A) Jail time

(B) Community service

(C) Court-mandated counseling

(D) Penalty fees

26. The Pregnancy Discrimination Act applies to none of the following parties except:

(A) Anyone over the age of 40

(B) All individuals with disabilities

(C) Women who are pregnant

(D) Women earning higher wages than men

27. Individuals who are deployed for military service, leave for basic training, leave for regularly scheduled training with the United States military, or are otherwise pulled away from civilian employment duties due to their service in the United States military must be afforded which of the following privileges when returning to their civilian job?

(A) Be given a position within the company but not necessarily the same job they once held

(B) Be required to start from scratch when they return and not necessarily find a job when they get there

(C) Be penalized by losing promotions and salaries

(D) Be treated as if they never left their position and therefore be eligible for all the same rights that would have been provided to them had they never left

28. Under the Worker Adjustment and Retraining Notification Act, manufacturing plants that are scheduled for major layoffs and those that have more than 100 employees are required to give individuals a minimum of how many days prior to layoffs or plant closings?

(A) 30

(B) 60

(C) 90

(D) 120

29. The organization that federally regulates advanced work opportunities and is responsible for improving work conditions as a means of creating good work conditions internationally is known as:

(A) The International Labor Organization

(B) The National Labor Relations Board

(C) The Securities and Exchange Commission

(D) The Merit System Protection Board

30. The United States organization that is responsible for overseeing and enforcing health and safety practices in the workplace is known as:

(A) The National Labor Relations Board

(B) The Veterans' Employment Training Service

(C) The Occupational Safety and Health Administration

(D) The Equal Employment Opportunity Commission

31. Which division of the United States Department of Justice is responsible for enforcing the laws against discrimination against individuals based on their disability, gender, national origin, race, or religion?

(A) Antitrust division

(B) Civil rights division

(C) Criminal division

(D) Justice management division

32. When a business is purchased by another company, the company that does the purchasing is known as:

(A) The acquisitioned company

(B) Business merger

(C) Business acquisition

(D) The acquiring company

33. In order to outline the long-term goals of a business, a model analyzing, designing, developing, implementing, and evaluating may be used. This method is known as:

(A) The Freemium model

(B) The ADDIE model

(C) The brick-and-mortar model

(D) The e-commerce model

34. When support is given to another, this is known as:

(A) Advocacy

(B) Alliance

(C) Appraisal

(D) Appeal

35. Money that is given to an individual as compensation for work-related expenses is known as:

(A) A bonus

(B) A wage

(C) An allowance

(D) A salary

36. When a financial valuation is placed on a business, this is known as:

(A) Appraisal

(B) Sale

(C) Auction

(D) Repossession

37. When an individual is given a job overseas working for a company, that position is known as:

(A) A vertical promotion

(B) An assignment

(C) A demotion

(D) A hiatus

38. When an organization is experiencing a loss of employees, this is known as:

(A) Consolidation

(B) Employment surplus

(C) Attrition

(D) Recruitment

39. The set starting pay for a given position is known as:

(A) Minimum wage

(B) Hazard pay

(C) Base pay

(D) Allowances

40. A group of benefits that may be offered to employees in addition to their base salary is known as:

(A) Pension plan

(B) Employment package

(C) Severance package

(D) Benefits program

41. A time in which employees are limited or restricted on making changes to or accessing their benefits, compensation, stock options, or other employment-based benefits is known as:

(A) Blackout period

(B) Open enrollment

(C) Fiscal period

(D) Best practice

42. An HR briefing is used for:

(A) Laying off employees

(B) Sharing information

(C) Growing support

(D) Managing expectations

43. The natural progression and advancement of a career is known as:

(A) Retirement planning

(B) Professional development

(C) Career-ladder promotion

(D) Training and retention

44. A career plateau is defined as:

(A) Reaching a career point where there is nowhere else to rise

(B) Climbing the career ladder to the top

(C) Becoming officially accredited in a field of employment

(D) Taking every opportunity to excel on the job

45. A method of training new employees or educating existing employees and supporting staff is known as:

(A) Write-up

(B) Commendation

(C) Citation

(D) Coaching

46. Which of the following terms best labels a structure within an organization that outlines the people in charge, starting from entry-level positions up to higher management or the reverse?

(A) Chain of command

(B) Evidentiary support

(C) Chain of custody

(D) Accentual support

47. Contingent workers are described as:

(A) Individuals who are employed to do a specific job during a set time frame

(B) Individuals who work on an as-needed basis and are paid a salary rather than an hourly wage

(C) Individuals who are not employed by the company but rather contracted to do a very specifically outlined job in a set time frame

(D) Individuals who are on call and respond on an as-needed basis only

48. The values, rules, processes, procedures, and expectations an organization has are known as its:

(A) Social culture

(B) Corporate culture

(C) Economic culture

(D) Political culture

49. A pay increase that is based on economic changes in a given area is known as:

(A) Cost of living

(B) Hazardous conditions

(C) Assignment allowance

(D) Hiring incentive

50. Specific requirements in order to meet the minimum standards for a job are known as:

(A) Standard of care

(B) Criterion

(C) Minimum requirements

(D) Intelligence training

51. A business whose dealings cross one or more countries' borders is known as:

(A) Cross-training

(B) International dealings

(C) Cross-border training

(D) International assignment

52. A higher rate of pay for an individual or additional pay that is given to an employee either for working in a high-risk area or for handling hazardous materials is known as:

(A) An incentive bonus

(B) A merit premium

(C) An assigns allowance

(D) A danger premium

53. A program designed to allow employees to put money into their retirement funds but not pay taxes on that fund until it is withdrawn at the time of retirement is known as:

(A) A 401k plan

(B) A severance package

(C) A deferred compensation plan

(D) A defined benefits plan

54. A training method that is implemented in a way that stretches out the training or educational process over an extended period of time is known as:

(A) Delayed training

(B) Distributed training

(C) Workforce pacing

(D) Employment summits

55. An analysis that places a financial value on aspects of a business that would otherwise not have a monetary value is known as:

(A) Property appraisal

(B) Insurance valuation estimate

(C) Economic valuation

(D) Property estimate

56. Non-salaried compensations that are offered to employees as part of a hiring package and often as an additional incentive to a salary are known as:

(A) Training

(B) Professional development

(C) Benefits

(D) Continued education

57. A business' ability to keep employees is known as:

(A) Employee retention

(B) Employee relations

(C) Employer branding

(D) Employee turnover

58. The way that a business presents itself to the community and general public is known as:

(A) Company outreach

(B) Employer branding

(C) Global responsibility

(D) Employer responsibility

59. Efforts made on the part of a business to improve the general public's perception of it is known as:

(A) Employment branding

(B) Product branding

(C) Investment branding

(D) Political branding

60. Avoiding or preventing international corruption, bribery, or other illegal activities as pertains to business is known as:

(A) Global ethics policy

(B) International trade deal

(C) Overseas embargo

(D) Globalization

61. A formal complaint most often filed with a company or organization's HR department against an employee, member of management, or client of the business is known as:

(A) A commendation

(B) A grievance

(C) A dispute

(D) An alienation

62. When one or more coworkers are harassing another and such harassment is creating a tense or uncomfortable environment, this is known as:

(A) Hostile work environment harassment

(B) Being unfit for employment

(C) Workplace sexual harassment

(D) A mob mentality

63. Individuals who are employed under a contract to do a specific job that is to be completed within a specific time frame and for a set salary are known as:

(A) Independent contractors

(B) Employment ambassadors

(C) Intellectual proprietors

(D) Subcontracted employees

64. What is the name of the legal protection granted to individuals who are not typically covered by a copyright, patent, or trademark?

(A) Trademark

(B) Intellectual property

(C) Patent

(D) Copyright

65. Skills individuals possess that help them communicate and build healthy relationships with others in a social setting are known as:

(A) Introverted skills

(B) Interpersonal skills

(C) Extroverted skills

(D) Both A and C

66. An insurance policy that some individuals and businesses seek to protect or reimburses them in the event of a kidnapping for ransom is known as:

(A) Life insurance policy

(B) Cost-of-doing-business insurance

(C) Kidnap-and-ransom insurance

(D) Investment capital insurance

67. When an organization invests in he learning and growth of its employees, this is called:

(A) Hiring

(B) Continued development

(C) Staying the course

(D) Layoffs

68. A learning model that is used to look at how an organization implements training, continued education, and the development of employees is known as:

(A) E-learning portals

(B) Learning effectiveness model

(C) Learning management systems

(D) Blended learning classrooms

69. A partnership that is created when two or more parties come together and assume equal or shared risk and responsibilities as well as rewards on a new shared business venture is known as:

(A) A sole proprietorship

(B) A joint venture

(C) A corporate merger

(D) An acquisitions sale

70. When an employer either temporarily or permanently loses employees due to a reduction on the business side, this is known as:

(A) Promotions

(B) Layoffs

(C) Vacations

(D) Strikes

71. A learning portal is an internet-based pathway to what?

(A) Education

(B) Training

(C) Career development

(D) All of the above

72. Benefits that are required to be provided by an employer to employees under the law are known as:

(A) Voluntary benefits

(B) Merit compensation

(C) Mandatory benefits

(D) Retirement benefits

73. When an employer uses an experienced individual to oversee, share experience, and provide insight to other employees, this individual is known as:

(A) A trainer

(B) An instructor

(C) A mentor

(D) A superior

74. The legal minimum amount a business can pay an employee under federal law is known as:

(A) Base pay

(B) Minimum wage

(C) Assignees' compensation

(D) Merit pay

75. A bonus given to an employee who agrees to relocate for a job is known as:

(A) An incentive bonus

(B) An increased mobility premium

(C) A mobility premium

(D) A pension premium

76. The technical term used when a business moves operations to another country in order to take advantage of cheaper labor or operating costs is:

(A) Venture capital

(B) International dealings

(C) Offshoring

(D) Income planning

77. When an employee moves up a career ladder, this advancement is known as:

(A) Hiring

(B) Promoting

(C) Firing

(D) Retiring

78. When individuals are given an increase in salary due to job performance, seniority, or other similar valuations of their employment, this pay increase is known as a:

(A) Bonus

(B) Salary

(C) Base pay

(D) Raise

79. Warning signs, physical or otherwise, that prompt a hiring manager to do more research into an applicant's background are known as:

(A) Reference checks

(B) Credentials

(C) Red flags

(D) Certification

80. When an organization pays to move an employee to another location for work purposes, this is known as:

(A) Relocation services

(B) Temp services

(C) Retirement services

(D) Employment service

81. A measure that outlines the potential financial outcome of a business venture and how long it will take to recoup the money initially invested is known as:

(A) A stock portfolio

(B) Start-up costs

(C) A return on investment

(D) Annual profit margins

82. A lump sum payment that is arranged to be given to an employee when an individual is laid off or fired is known as a/an:

(A) Hiring bonus

(B) Incentive bonus

(C) Severance package

(D) Compensation package

83. Social interactions for the purpose of sharing common interests are known as:

(A) Social networking

(B) Social-emotional connections

(C) Social distancing

(D) Social structures

84. The start of a new business venture is known as a/an:

(A) Start-up

(B) Acquisition

(C) Merger

(D) Take-over

85. When employees may work from home or otherwise work remotely, this is known as:

(A) Telecommuting

(B) Remote employment

(C) Intranet facilitation

(D) E-commerce employment

86. Ensuring that a company and its employees are in compliance with company policies and procedures, as well as local, state, and federal laws, is part of which type of duty?

(A) Administrative

(B) Operational

(C) Social

(D) Strategic

87. When an employer pays part or all of the tuition for employees' continued education, this is known as:

(A) Scholarship

(B) Tuition

(C) Grants

(D) Reimbursement

88. The span between the lowest and highest salary for a career is known as:

(A) Wage band

(B) Compensation

(C) Minimum wage

(D) Convenience

89. Information, developmental methods, or physical materials are generally contractually owned by the business an employee worked for when creating them. This is known as:

(A) Trademark

(B) Copyright

(C) Proprietary

(D) Intellectual property

90. The specific amount of time that the HR department or other departments in a business are required to keep documents and hard copies of information for either business purposes or legal purposes is known as:

(A) Record retention schedule

(B) Employee information database

(C) Recertification information

(D) Trial period

91. The process of attracting qualified employment candidates to fill positions in a business is known as:

(A) Advertising

(B) Recruitment

(C) Interviewing

(D) Hiring

92. The process of confirming an employee's professional history and gathering information about the individual in question is known as:

(A) Application process

(B) Employment history

(C) Reference check

(D) Background check

93. An employee who moves back home after working in a position abroad is an example of:

(A) Commuting

(B) Relocating

(C) Assimilating

(D) Repatriation

94. When an employee is given a specific set amount of time off from work to study, relax, rest, or travel while still receiving pay, this type of leave of absence is known as:

    (A) Sick leave

    (B) Sabbatical leave

    (C) PTO time

    (D) Vacation time

95. When an individual is subjected to unwanted sexual behaviors, this behavior is known as:

    (A) Verbal harassment

    (B) Sexual harassment

    (C) Physical harassment

    (D) Emotional harassment

96. Employees who work internationally can be paid in two currencies under which payroll format?

    (A) Delayed payroll

    (B) Split payroll

    (C) Daily payroll

    (D) Flex payroll

97. A business that is able to generate revenue and maintain or increase revenue is seeing evidence of:

    (A) Growth

    (B) Sustainability

    (C) Revenue

    (D) Investment

98. An employment practice in which the employee is permanently employed and cannot be simply fired is known as:

(A) Independent contracting

(B) Tenure

(C) Seniority

(D) Outsource contracting

99. A process that is used by HR personnel as a means of collecting feedback is known as:

(A) 360-degree

(B) Employee survey

(C) 180-degree

(D) Employer survey

100. If a business is purchased in a way that will allow the owners to essentially open the doors and begin operations almost immediately, this is known as:

(A) New build

(B) Turnkey

(C) Operational

(D) Renovated

Test 1 Answers

1. (D) Performance

   Managing a business and its employees, understanding the inner workings of a business, and understanding the work of the employees is all part of the role HR plays in the performance of a business.

2. (C) Line management

   Line management refers to the main parts of a business that generate money, or revenue. Most often this refers to the manufacture of products, sales, or services offered. These things bring money into an organization.

3. (A) Organizational development

   Organizational development is a process that is used to improve the way businesses function.

4. (C) A small business

   Generally speaking, a fully functioning HR department will manage six key points of business operations: HR operations, recruitment and selection, compensation and benefits, HR development and retention, employee relations, and risk management.

5. (B) For employee health and safety

   The Occupational Safety and Health Administration is a federal organization that sets standards and laws that businesses and organizations must follow to ensure the overall health and safety of the employees who work for them.

6. (B) Training

   HR must advertise for open positions within an organization or business, screen applicants and the information provided as part of the application process, and interview potential employment candidates. Training does not occur until after an employee has been hired to work for a business.

7. (A) The interview process

   HR personnel are tasked with receiving all employment applications, vetting the applicants to determine which ones meet the basic qualifications to adequately fill the position, narrowing down qualified applicants, and choosing which candidates are right for the position.

8. (D) The size of the HR department required

   A small business does not require a comprehensive HR department. The larger the HR department, the larger the company should be, and the more tasks that HR department should be able to take on.

9. (C) OSHA is responsible for ensuring the overall health and safety of employees.

   OSHA officials periodically check business compliance, cite businesses that fail to comply, and ensure that measures are taken to protect the health and safety of employees in all industries.

10. (B) Advertisements

   Advertising means informing the public of positions within a business that need to be filled as a means of enticing qualified candidates to apply.

11. (D) All of the above

   Once hired, employees go through orientation, which familiarizes them with an organization's policies and procedures, mission statement, and overall purpose. Following orientation, employees are trained to ensure that they understand the finer points of the job that they have been hired to do.

   The longer employees are with an organization, the more they will be given opportunities to continue their education in order to better serve the business. All three of these components play a key role in employee success and retention, as well as the input those employees offer.

12. (A) Americans with Disabilities Act

Under the Americans with Disabilities Act, employers are required to make reasonable accommodations so that employees with disabilities may do their jobs. The law states that reasonable accommodations cannot cause undue hardship to the employer or organization.

13. (D) 40

Per the Age Discrimination in Employment Act, any employee who is under the age of 40 does not qualify for age discrimination.

14. (A) The Consolidated Omnibus Budget Reconciliation Act

Under the Consolidated Omnibus Budget Reconciliation Act (COBRA), employees may continue their health-care insurance coverage for a specific time if they are not on the job. In many cases, employees are required to pay part or all of their health-care premiums during this time.

15. (C) Pay their typical insurance premiums

Employees who are temporarily out of work but still employed have the right to seek COBRA insurance. In order to maintain their insurance during this time, employees are most often required to pay the premiums for insurance out of pocket while out of work.

16. (D) The Wall Street Reform and Consumer Protection Act

The Dodd-Frank Wall Street Reform and Consumer Protection Act affords several protections under federal law, including but not limited to golden parachutes, Sa-on-Pay, and Say-on-Pay frequency.

17. (C) The Department of Labor

The United States Department of Labor is responsible for setting the guidelines and enforcing the law under the Employee Retirement Income Security Act.

18. (A) FMLA

    The Family and Medical Leave Act is most often referred to as FMLA.

19. (D) The Fair Labor Standards Act

    Under the Fair Labor Standards Act, the United States government outlines the legal minimum wage, required pay for overtime worked, and child labor laws.

20. (C) The Genetic Information Nondiscrimination Act

    Under the Genetic Information Nondiscrimination Act, health insurance companies are not allowed to deny coverage or charge more money for coverage based solely on the fact that someone has a genetic predisposition to a health condition.

21. (D) HIPAA

    The Health Insurance Portability and Accountability Act is most commonly referred to by the acronym HIPAA.

22. (B) I-9

    During the hiring process, an I-9 form is completed in order to verify that an individual is legally eligible to work within the borders of the United States.

23. (A) The Department of Labor

    The United States Department of Labor is responsible for implementing and enforcing the Occupational Safety and Health Act, which is regulated through the Division of Occupational Safety and Health Administration.

24. (B) The Patient Protection and Affordability Care Act

The Patient Protection and Affordability Care Act is most often referred to as Obamacare after the president who implemented it. The act used to require that all individuals purchase health-care coverage. This law requires employers to offer health insurance coverage to all employees and penalizes those who do not.

25. (D) Penalty fees

Any individual who failed to purchase health-care insurance used to be charged a penalty. This has now changed.

26. (C) Women who are pregnant

The only individuals who are granted protection under the Pregnancy Discrimination Act are pregnant women or women who develop a condition during pregnancy or immediately after childbirth.

27. (D) Be treated as if they never left their position and therefore be eligible for all the same rights that would have been provided to them had they never left

Under the Uniformed Services Employment and Reemployment Rights Act, employers are required to reinstate military employees to the positions that they left and ensure that their compensation, benefits, seniority, and opportunities for promotion match their time with the company as if they had never left for service.

28. (B) 60

The Worker Adjustment and Retraining Notification Act requires that employers provide at least 60 days' notice prior to significant layoffs. This law was enacted to give employees time to find other employment or make other arrangements for themselves in the event that major layoffs or plant closures occur in their communities.

29. (A) The International Labor Organization

The International Labor Organization is designed to promote good working conditions that are conducive to freedom, equality, security, and the support of human dignity for men and women throughout the world.

30. (C) The Occupational Safety and Health Administration

The Occupational Safety and Health Administration is responsible for ensuring the overall safety and health of the workplace for employees.

31. (B) Civil rights division

The United States Department of Justice, under the Division of Civil Rights, is responsible for enforcing laws against those who discriminate against an individual's civil rights. These civil rights include but are not limited to disability, gender, national origin, race, or religion.

32. (D) The acquiring company

In business dealings, the company that is purchasing a property, business, organization, or other such entity is known as the acquiring company.

33. (B) The ADDIE model

ADDIE requires an initial analysis, a design for what a company is looking for, a process for developing that business model, the implementation of that business model, and an evaluation of the effectiveness of the model.

34. (A) Advocacy

In business, when support is given on behalf of an individual or party, this is known as advocacy.

35. (C) An allowance

When an employer allots money for an employee to use for work-related expenses, this is known as an allowance.

36. (A) Appraisal

An appraisal is the review of a property or business in order to place a financial value on that entity. Most often an appraisal is done by a real estate professional.

37. (B) An assignment

When an employer offers a position outside an employee's typical country of employment, that job is referred to as an assignment. You most often hear this term in regard to journalism: "I'm on assignment in ..."

38. (C) Attrition

Attrition is when there is a loss of employees within a company. Attrition can occur because the current employees have contracts that have come to an end, employees are resigning or retiring, and/or the entity is experiencing a high volume of employees with illnesses or other reasons for leaving the company.

39. (C) Base pay

Base pay is a set salary for a given position of employment. The base pay is determined by evaluating the market for similar positions to arrive at a fair and competitive salary.

40. (D) Benefits program

A benefits program is a set of items, in addition to a salary, that an employer may offer employees as part of the compensation for their employment. A benefits package may include things such as a 401k plan, stock options, health-care insurance, short-term disability, long-term disability, and fitness club memberships.

41. (A) Blackout period

A blackout period is a term used in business to describe a set time period in which employees are unable to make changes to their benefits and compensation packages. They may not have access to them at all during this time.

42. (B) Sharing information

A briefing is the gathering and sharing of important information in a business. Briefings can be shared throughout an organization or strictly with select individuals or groups.

43. (C) Career-ladder promotion

A career-ladder promotion is the strategic way that an individual advances within a field, starting when the person is first employed and continuing on for as long as the employee remains with a company and progresses in his/her career.

44. (A) Reaching a career point where there is nowhere else to rise

A career plateau occurs when a person has nowhere higher to go in a particular position or particular field because he/she has reached the pinnacle of success with a particular organization.

45. (D) Coaching

Coaching tracks training, education, and refreshment of existing policies and procedures.

46. (A) Chain of command

Chain of command is the structure of authority within an organization. For example, a typical business structure might be as follows, from the top down: CEO, director of operations, senior managers, team leaders, team members. In this example, the CEO would be the highest level of authority, and team members (entry-level employees) would be the lowest.

47. (A) Individuals who are employed to do a specific job during a set time frame

Contingent workers are required to complete the assigned work within a designated time frame. Contingent workers are generally hired to do a specific job or produce a specific product. Once the job is complete and the contract is satisfied, the employees are most often released from the company that they were working through.

48. (B) Corporate culture

Corporate culture is the way a company acts and the views that it has. This includes business values, corporate rules, production processes, and company-based procedures.

49. (A) Cost of living

A cost-of-living raise is determined by the location of the facility, the increase in employees' cost of living, and the prosperity of the local community.

50. (B) Criterion

Criterion refers to a specific set of requirements that are needed in order for an employee to meet basic minimum standards. An example of a criterion might be that an individual is required to possess an associate's degree in order to be hired for a position.

51. (C) Cross-border training

Cross-border training is when an organization conducts business that crosses one or more countries' borders. Cross-border training can occur on the same continent or worldwide, such as when a business has a home office in New York, a production facility in New Mexico, and a satellite business in Dubai.

52. (D) A danger premium

An employer will often pay what is known as a danger premium to employees who work in what is considered a high-risk field or who are put into a job that is located in an area that is considered to put their lives in imminent danger. Working with hazardous materials, working in a war zone, or working in an otherwise unsafe environment are all examples of circumstances in which an employer may pay a danger premium to employees.

53. (C) A deferred compensation plan

A deferred compensation plan is an employee's retirement or pension plan that allows employees, who pay into the retirement fund over the life of their careers, to withdraw the money from that fund upon their retirement. The money is not taxed until it is withdrawn from the account.

54. (B) Distributed training

Distributed training is a method used by businesses and organizations to implement training or professional development over an extended period of time, both in person and through e-learning. It allows employees to absorb smaller amounts of information at a time, preventing them from being overwhelmed.

55. (C) Economic valuation

An economic valuation will generally include placing a value on things such as the air quality around a factory, groundwater supply's quality, or a business' carbon footprint. These items can increase the value of a property or decrease it despite not being a physical part of the property.

56. (C) Benefits

Employee benefits refer to non-salaried compensation given to employees as part of their employment package. This compensation can include medical insurance, dental insurance, vision insurance, 401ks or pension plans, reimbursements for continued employment education or training, work-related expense allowances, work-related expense reimbursements, or allowances for working abroad. Employee benefits, while not monetary, incentivize employees to want to work for the company versus taking a job offer from another organization.

57. (A) Employee retention

Employee retention refers to a business' ability to keep employees. Some key points to ensuring that employees want to stay with a company include ensuring people feel satisfied in their jobs, are fairly compensated for the work they are doing, have a sense of accomplishment for the work that they do, and feel heard by their employers.

58. (B) Employer branding

Employer branding is defined as an organization's active efforts to represent itself to the community and general public. This includes community outreach, branding, stockholders, shareholders, and end customers.

59. (A) Employment branding

Employment branding is the efforts of a business to change or improve the general public's perception of it. Efforts like this are most often made in order for a business to improve the chances of being recognized as an employer of choice, thereby attracting more highly qualified job candidates.

60. (A) Global ethics policy

Global ethics policies are internationally set guidelines designed to help prevent corruption, bribery, and other illegal activity when organizations work on an international scale.

61. (B) A grievance

A grievance occurs when employees file a formal complaint, generally through the HR department or a member of management, against another employee, upper management, or client.

62. (A) Hostile work environment harassment

Hostile work environment harassment occurs when an employee or multiple employees harass another individual.

63. (A) Independent contractors

Independent contractors are individuals hired to do an extremely specific job under a set schedule for a set fee. When the employment tasks under the contract are complete, the contract is concluded.

64. (B) Intellectual property

Intellectual property is ownership that is recognized from a legal standpoint as it pertains to ideas, creations, inventions, or other similar scopes that generally come from an individual's mind and are not typically covered under a copyright, patent, or trademark.

65. (B) Interpersonal skills

Interpersonal skills allow people to build healthy relationships through strong and confident communication that ultimately results in positive professional relationships in the workplace.

66. (C) Kidnap-and-ransom insurance

Kidnap-and-ransom insurance protects individuals, businesses, organizations, business owners, and employees in the event of a kidnapping. The insurance policy reimburses the cost of the ransom. These policies are usually sought by organizations in high-risk parts of the world.

67. (B) Continued Development

Continued development of employees is necessary for the growth of an organizations as well as for enhancing career growth for its employees.

68. (B) Learning effectiveness model

A learning effectiveness model looks at the program and processes that a business utilizes in order to train, further educate, professionally develop, and otherwise improve the education and training of new and existing employees in an organization. The ultimate goal of such training is to help a business run more effectively and meet its long-term goals.

69. (B) A joint venture

A joint venture is a business partnership between two or more parties. The parties involved assume a shared risk and reward by partaking in such a business venture. In the event that the venture fails, both parties will lose everything that they invested. In the event that the venture succeeds, both parties will split the profits and rewards.

70. (B) Layoffs

Layoffs are either a temporary or permanent loss of employees. Layoffs most often occur when a company is struggling financially or being purchased by another company. Layoffs may also occur during a slow holiday season, with employees rehired when things pick up, or they can be more permanent, such as if a company shuts down.

71. (D) All of the above

A learning portal is an internet-based pathway that employees can utilize to complete training and take advantage of career development opportunities. Online learning portals are utilized by businesses because of their ability to provide accountability and flexibility in the education and training of employees, furthering their development and helping them climb their respective career ladders.

72. (C) Mandatory benefits

Mandatory benefits are required to be provided by an employer to employees under the law.

73. (C) A mentor

A mentor is someone who has extensive work experience and assists new employees by guiding them and sharing knowledge.

74. (B) Minimum wage

Under United States federal law, the minimum wage is the lowest amount any business is allowed to pay employees.

75. (C) A mobility premium

A mobility premium is a bonus given to employees in addition to their salary for being willing to work in another country.

76. (C) Offshoring

Offshoring refers to a business that moves its operations to another country due to lower labor, supply, and operation costs.

77. (B) Promoting

Promotions require employees to take on more responsibility and often offer an increase in salary. They are considered an advancement on an individual's career ladder.

78. (D) Raise

A raise is generally given to an individual for reasons including job performance, time on the job, annual reviews, seniority within a company, etc.

79. (C) Red flags

Red flags are anything that appears on an application, in reference checks, or in the interviewing process that makes an interviewer think that information needs to be more thoroughly checked.

80. (A) Relocation services

An employer provides relocation services to employees in order to move them from their current homes to new locations in another town, state, or country. In addition to physically moving these employees, employers may also assist with finding a realtor in the new location, finding a rental home, or purchasing a new home, or help with deposits and other financial matters related to moving for the job.

81. (C) A return on investment

A return on investment measures the amount of money that an individual or group puts into a business and the amount of time required for that business to generate enough money to return that sum to the individual.

82. (C) Severance package

A severance package is a special arrangement of payments and other compensations as a final concession to employees at the time they are laid off or fired.

83. (A) Social networking

The business world uses social networking to build contacts, advertise, expand the business, etc.

84. (A) Start-up

A start-up is the term for a new business venture. This includes the development, investments, and start-up operations.

85. (A) Telecommuting

Telecommuting is the process of working remotely or from home through a computer or other electronic device.

86. (B) Operational

Ensuring that a business is in compliance with the law is vital to that organization's success. Failure to follow regulations could lead to severe penalties. Ensuring compliance is HR's responsibility.

87. (D) Reimbursement

Tuition reimbursement is a benefit that is offered by some employers to pay a portion or all of employees' educational costs as related to their employment.

88. (A) Wage band

A wage band refers to the span between the highest and lowest wages for any field of employment.

89. (C) Proprietary

Information, developmental methods, or physical materials are typically not owned by the person who created them but by the company they were created under.

90. (A) Record retention schedule

A record retention schedule is a set amount of time that a business or HR department is legally required to keep important documents and hard copies of information. Once the time period for record retention has passed, businesses are permitted to destroy or delete the information.

91. (B) Recruitment

Recruitment is the process of advertising and otherwise attracting qualified candidates to apply for vacant jobs in a business.

92. (C) Reference check

A reference check confirms an employment candidate's professional work history and abilities.

93. (D) Repatriation

When an employee returns home after working abroad, this move is known as repatriation.

94. (B) Sabbatical leave

Sabbatical leave happens when an employer gives an employee a set amount of paid time off.

95. (B) Sexual harassment

Sexual harassment is, by definition, unwelcomed sexually motivated behavior. It can be verbal, visual, or sexual in nature.

96. (B) Split payroll

Split payroll allows employees who work internationally to split the currency in which they are paid. A portion of the employees' pay can be paid in the currency of their home nation, and the other portion can be paid in the currency of the country in which they are working.

97. (B) Sustainability

Sustainability is a business' ability to start, maintain, and increase revenue.

98. (B) Tenure

Tenure means a permanent job that has renewals at set intervals for the life of the contract. Employees with tenure are incredibly difficult to fire unless they are found to be in breach of contract.

99. (A) 360-degree

This is a process used in HR as a means of collecting internal and external information to assess a business' practices. Feedback is collected from employees of all levels, including entry-level, middle management, and upper management, as well as customers and suppliers.

100. (B) Turnkey

A home or business is considered to be "turnkey" when it is purchased and can be used or lived in immediately.

Test 2 (100 Questions)

1. Money that is needed for a start-up venture is known as:

    (A) Venture capital

    (B) Upfront costs

    (C) Seasonal costs

    (D) Acquisitions capital

2. Human resources has three key functions. Which of the following is not the responsibility of the HR department?

    (A) Administrative duties

    (B) Strategic duties

    (C) Operational duties

    (D) Securing capital for start-ups

3. The typical amount of time that it takes an HR department to fill a vacant position in a business is referred to as:

    (A) Duration of vacancy

    (B) Layoffs

    (C) Time to fill

    (D) Employment retention

4. Keeping detailed records for the HR department is part of:

    (A) Operational duties

    (B) Strategic duties

    (C) Administrative duties

    (D) Employee relation duties

5. A tax policy afforded to international employees that arranges for taxes to be paid, with a portion going to both the employee's native country and the country the person is working in, is known as:

(A) International employment policy

(B) Tax equalization policy

(C) International e-commerce policy

(D) Fair tax policy

6. What are individuals known as when they hold a financial interest in an organization?

(A) Shareholders

(B) Investors

(C) Partners

(D) Stakeholders

7. S.M.A.R.T is a method of setting and reaching goals in an organization. The S.M.A.R.T acronym includes for all of the following except:

(A) Specific

(B) Action

(C) Oriented

(D) Timeless

8. A way of assessing employees to determine if they are qualified to fill a vacant position in a business is known as:

(A) Screening tools

(B) Social networking

(C) Behavioral interview

(D) Employee assessment

9. Specific limits that are placed on employees' stocks for the company that they work for, which restricts the time frame in which they can offload those stocks, is known as:

   (A) Severance packages

   (B) Limited liabilities

   (C) Restricted stock

   (D) Return on investment

10. Paying back borrowed funds is also known as:

   (A) Financial loans

   (B) Gifts and gratuities

   (C) Bonuses and compensation

   (D) Reimbursements

11. A set of skills, abilities, or knowledge that an individual needs in order to qualify for a specific position is known as:

   (A) Education

   (B) Training

   (C) Qualifications

   (D) Development

12. A process that specifically focuses on assisting a business with its planning, implementing, and organizing is known as:

   (A) Organizational development

   (B) Management development

   (C) Career development

   (D) Educational development

13. An undeniable sense of what is right and wrong is known as:

(A) Behavioral guidance

(B) Moral repugnance

(C) Moral absolute

(D) Undeniable truth

14. If an employee prefers to take jobs within an organization that have mobility, this means:

(A) The employee wants to stay in the same location and the same job.

(B) The employee has a position that requires him/her to drive around the community.

(C) The employee must commute more than 30 minutes each day.

(D) The employee is willing to relocate nationally or internationally for work.

15. When a business raises pay for employees for reaching goals related to their job performance, this is known as:

(A) Performance review

(B) Merit increase

(C) Incentive bonus

(D) Severance pay

16. Research that is done by a business in order to determine the average pay for any given job on the market is known as:

(A) Minimum wage

(B) Market salary survey

(C) Base wage survey

(D) Hazard pay

17. Compensation that is made through a single payment is known as:

    (A) Lump sum compensation

    (B) Staggered payment

    (C) Delayed compensation

    (D) Return on investment

18. A business model that looks at a business' programs as they pertain to training, employee development, etc. is known as:

    (A) An e-learning model

    (B) A learning effectiveness model

    (C) A blended learning model

    (D) A transitional education model

19. When individuals in an organization come together with the common goal of gaining better wages, benefits, compensation, or better working conditions, this is known as:

    (A) Labor board

    (B) Employee activists

    (C) Labor union

    (D) Employment strike

20. An internet-based pathway that some employers choose to utilize as an access point for their employees to continue their education and training resources in the company is known as:

    (A) Intranet

    (B) Server

    (C) Circuit board

    (D) CCTV

21. When a business invests in management teams by continuing to offer them development and training opportunities, preparing them to move up career ladders in the company, this is known as:

(A) Leadership development

(B) Entry-level training

(C) Exit interviews

(D) Blended learning

22. When multiple parties join together in a shared partnership, this is known as:

(A) Sole proprietorship

(B) Joint venture

(C) Limited liability corporation

(D) Partnership

23. An international assignee is defined as:

(A) An individual who is hired to do a job in a different country

(B) A company that operates on more than one continent and in more than one country

(C) An individual who agrees to work outside his/her native country

(D) An ambassador used to greet any clients or business associates from abroad

24. When an employer chooses to use an existing employee to complete a task, this strategy is known as:

(A) Outsourcing

(B) Contract employment

(C) Insourcing

(D) Abuse of powers

25. Compensation, either financial or non-financial, given to an employee to motivate, incentivize, or persuade is known as:

(A) Bonuses

(B) Benefits

(C) Incentives

(D) Amenities

26. Compensation an employer may give an employee due to dangerous living conditions or working conditions is known as:

(A) Hazard pay

(B) Merit bonus

(C) Employment incentive

(D) Hardship premium

27. Which of the following definitions correctly matches the term "greenfield operations"?

(A) A corporation's mindset to be green and earth-friendly

(B) Named after the man who created recycling and repurposing of materials on a global scale

(C) A way for business start-ups to analyze potential outcomes for new business ventures

(D) When a business builds all new facilities on newly purchased land

28. The United States legal system defines the relationship between the employees of a business and their employer as:

(A) Employment branding

(B) Equity partnership

(C) Employment at will

(D) Globalization

29. The responsibility of a business in regard to the effects it has on the environment and the local community is known as:

(A) Environmental protection

(B) Environmental neglect

(C) Environmental responsibility

(D) Environmental restoration

30. An essential component of HR refers to employee communication among employees, management, and the overall chain of command. This is known as:

(A) Employer relations

(B) Business relations

(C) Cultural relations

(D) Employee relations

31. When the HR department or personnel allow certain information about an employee to be accessed by that employee in order to make changes or updates, this is known as:

(A) Personnel documents

(B) Employee self-service

(C) Employment at will

(D) Personnel files

32. When a business reduces the number of employees, this is known as:

(A) Downsizing

(B) Infrastructure

(C) Streamlining

(D) Capitalizing

33. A method of professional development in which all learning is done online through a program that tracks employees' progress and determines when they have successfully completed the program is known as:

(A) In-class instruction

(B) E-learning

(C) Blended learning

(D) Delayed training

34. When personnel who work in the HR division of a business are specifically assigned to that department and do not work anywhere else, this is known as:

(A) Cross-training

(B) Distributed training

(C) Dedicated HR personnel

(D) Unilateral training

35. A retirement plan that sets up payment schedules in which the individual will receive retirement benefits is known as:

(A) A defined benefits plan

(B) A delayed benefits and compensation plan

(C) A deferred compensation plan

(D) A flex benefits plan

36. Written proof in the form of certifications, diplomas, or digital badges that show an individual has completed a certain course, exam, or training is known as:

(A) Certification

(B) References

(C) Credentials

(D) Training

37. A practice in which an employee that works in one particular department is additionally trained to do multiple jobs in other departments is known as:

(A) Basic training

(B) On-the-job training

(C) Cross-training

(D) Webinar training

38. What is it called when an organization works to positively impact the local community?

(A) International environmental protection

(B) Corporate citizenship

(C) Environmental Protection Agency

(D) Community outreach

39. The commitments that businesses make to their local communities are known as:

(A) Corporate economic responsibility

(B) Corporate fiscal responsibility

(C) Corporate social responsibility

(D) Corporate environmental responsibility

40. When individuals gain a certification or an educational degree after completing the necessary coursework to show their competency in a particular field or to be accredited, this is an example of:

(A) Penalization

(B) Affirmation

(C) Certification

(D) Aforementioned

41. When a group of servers is used, specifically by one business, in order to share content through the organization, this is known as:

(A) Cloud computing

(B) Designated server

(C) Encryption software

(D) Open forums

42. When a business ensures that the company and its employees are following company policies and procedures, as well as local, state, and federal laws, this is known as:

(A) Training

(B) Recertifying

(C) Compliance

(D) Decontaminating

43. Career planning is defined as all of the following except:

(A) Setting professional goals

(B) Evaluating how to reach those goals

(C) Taking advantage of career opportunities when they come along

(D) Accepting benefits and compensation when offered

44. A breakdown analysis uses ______ to analyze and categorize a business.

(A) Revenue sources

(B) Employee turnover

(C) Annual expenditures

(D) Supply and demand

45. When individuals or groups invest money into a business in order to financially have a stake in that business, this is known as:

(A) Buy-in

(B) Profit-sharing

(C) Stocks

(D) Bonuses

46. An individual, group, or entity that is chosen to receive the proceeds of a retirement plan or will is known as:

(A) Power of attorney

(B) Dependent

(C) Beneficiary

(D) Proxy

47. A method that provides the best outcome in a business is known as:

(A) Orientation and training

(B) Best practices

(C) Developmental opportunities

(D) Promotional advantages

48. Many employers have a software system that tracks the various stages of employment applications. This is called:

(A) Application process

(B) Application review

(C) Application tracking system

(D) Recruitment and HR resources

49. As part of the interview process, many employers conduct _______ to ensure that potential candidates are well screened before being offered employment.

(A) Background checks

(B) Security clearances

(C) Interviews

(D) Reference checks

50. An official method that employees can utilize to challenge a decision that has been made by their workplace or by members of management is known as:

(A) Arbitration

(B) Reconciliation

(C) Summary judgment

(D) Appeal

51. When an individual new to the field studies under an experienced person in order to gain knowledge, understanding, and experience, the individual is known as a/an:

(A) Understudy

(B) Apprentice

(C) Cohort

(D) Accomplice

52. A way to resolve a disagreement between two or more parties without utilizing formal or official legal proceedings is known as:

(A) Alternative dispute resolution

(B) Advocacy

(C) Affirmative action

(D) Allowance

53. Equal treatment utilized to level the playing field as it pertains to employment applications and employment candidates is known as:

(A) Arbitration

(B) Behavioral interview

(C) Affirmative action

(D) Benefits program

54. A method of accounting that businesses use to compare invoices paid to the income they have generated and the expenses they have had throughout the fiscal year is known as:

(A) Profitability

(B) Acquisitions

(C) Development

(D) Accrual

55. The organization responsible for enforcing labor laws in the United States is known as:

(A) The International Labor Organization

(B) The National Labor Relations Board

(C) The Occupational Safety and Health Administration

(D) The United States Commission on Civil Rights

56. The United States federal organization responsible for dealings and security in the business market is known as:

(A) The United States Department of Justice

(B) The United States Commission on Civil Rights

(C) The National Labor Relations Board

(D) The Securities and Exchange Commission

57. What act was passed to protect workers, employees' families, and communities in regard to major layoffs in a factory or plant setting?

(A) The Worker Adjustment and Retraining Notification Act

(B) The Uniformed Services Employment and Reemployment Rights Act

(C) The National Labor Relations Act

(D) The Fair Labor Standards Act

58. A federal government organization responsible for enforcing the standard for minimum wage, unemployment insurance, reemployment services, and occupational safety is known as:

(A) The Equal Employment Opportunity Commission

(B) The Federal Trade Commission

(C) The National Labor Relations Board

(D) The Department of Labor

59. Under the Pregnancy Discrimination Act, women are protected during all of the following except:

(A) Elective abortions

(B) Becoming pregnant

(C) An existing pregnancy

(D) Health-related conditions due to pregnancy

60. The Uniformed Services Employment and Reemployment Rights Act provides protection to:

(A) Underprivileged communities

(B) United States military service members

(C) Police officers and firefighters

(D) Government officials

61. The ____________ requires that workplaces be kept free of toxic chemicals, excessively dangerous noise levels, dangers related to machinery, exposure to excessively high or low temperatures, and unsanitary working conditions.

(A) Patient Protection and Affordable Care Act

(B) Occupational Safety and Health Act

(C) Ohio Pregnancy Discrimination Act

(D) Health Insurance Portability and Accountability Act

62. The Patient Protection and Affordable Care Act expands health coverage by:

(A) Lowering the cost of all public health insurance companies

(B) Mandating that private insurance be open to all individuals

(C) Expanding health-care coverage through public and private insurers, as well as expanding Medicare and Medicaid

(D) Expanding government health insurance coverage to include all United States citizens

63. The Immigration and Nationality Act applies to:

(A) Completing I-9 forms

(B) Immigration laws as they pertain to employment

(C) Targeting and deporting illegal immigrants

(D) Ensuring immigration and customs enforcement

64. Unfair wages or compensation, unsafe working conditions, or other similar grievances that an individual is subjected to because of his/her immigration status are illegal per the ________________.

(A) Immigration and Customs Enforcement Act

(B) Fair Wages Act

(C) Immigration and Nationality Act

(D) Fair Labor Standards Act

65. According to the Federal Labor Board, work hours can include but are not limited to all of the following except:

(A) Orientation and training

(B) Fitness workouts at employer facilities

(C) Mandatory rest periods

(D) Business dinners

66. Under the Genetic Information Nondiscrimination Act, employers may not discriminate against their employees in regard to hiring, firing, transferring, or promoting because of:

(A) A genetic predisposition to an illness

(B) A preexisting condition

(C) A chronic health issue that requires employees to take regular time off

(D) A terminal illness

67. The ________ states that individuals who work in the same or similar field, have the same knowledge and qualifications, and work under the same or similar working conditions may not be discriminated against based on their gender.

(A) Fair Credit Reporting Act

(B) Equal Pay Act

(C) Fair Labor Standards Act

(D) Occupational Safety and Health Act

68. Employees whose companies meet specific requirements are permitted under federal law to take up to 12 weeks off work in a rolling calendar year. This right falls under _________.

(A) The Ohio Pregnancy Discrimination Act

(B) The Maternity and Paternity Leave Act

(C) The United States Family and Medical Leave Act

(D) United States Civil Rights Act

69. The Dodd-Frank Wall Street Reform and Consumer Protection Act is administered, supervised and enforced by:

(A) The Securities and Exchange Commission

(B) The Internal Revenue Office

(C) the Department of Finance

(D) The American Exchange

70. The Dodd-Frank Wall Street Reform and Consumer Protection Act was created in order to:

(A) Create financial stability

(B) Create transparency

(C) Make publicly traded companies accountable

(D) All of the above

71. Under the Civil Rights Act of 1964, no employees may be discriminated against based on their race, color, religion, or national origin so long as the employer has at least ____.

(A) One or more employees

(B) More than 15 employees

(C) More than 50 employees

(D) More than 100 employees

72. The Consolidated Omnibus Budget Reconciliation Act is most commonly known as:

(A) COBRA

(B) FMLA

(C) ADA

(D) GINA

73. Which of the following laws prevents an employer from discriminating against employment candidates and active employees based on a disability, regardless of whether it is physical or mental?

(A) The Civil Rights Act of 1964

(B) The Americans with Disabilities Act

(C) The Equal Pay Act

(D) The Worker Adjustment and Retraining Notification Act

74. Any organization that has at least one employee with a disability must post _____ signs in an area that employees frequent.

(A) Minimum wage requirements

(B) Immigration

(C) Civil rights

(D) Americans with Disabilities rights

75. Performing thorough ________ ensures an employee is prepared to discharge the responsibilities of a job.

(A) Training

(B) Orientation

(C) Exit interviews

(D) Interviews

76. The Associate Professional in Human Resources credentials are valid for those seeking employment __________.

(A) In New York

(B) In the United States

(C) Anywhere internationally

(D) As contracted employees

77. HR departments facilitate:

(A) Business purchases

(B) Supply and sales

(C) Overall business success

(D) Profit and loss

78. The minimum amount of money that a business can pay an employee by law is known as:

(A) Minimum wage

(B) Benefits

(C) Wage cap

(D) Salary

79. A spreadsheet detailing the jobs in a business, the detailed workings of those jobs, and the skills an employment candidate needs to possess in order to be qualified for those jobs is called:

(A) Job analysis

(B) Pre-employment screening

(C) Job database

(D) Qualifications exam

80. Who is responsible for keeping a current summary of United States jobs and their estimated growth over time?

(A)The Department of Labor

(B)The Office of Unemployment Insurance

(C)The Occupational Safety and Health Administration

(D)The Bureau of Labor Statistics

81. Sole proprietorships, limited liability partnerships, limited liability companies, and corporations are:

(A) Global markets

(B) Business structures

(C) Employment positions

(D) Infrastructures

82. Part of the responsibilities of HR operations is to establish and enforce laws, guidelines, and rules for a business. This responsibility is known as:

(A) Compensation

(B) Compliance

(C) Corporation

(D) Condensation

83. A method of employee management and retention involving recruiting the best-qualified employees for the job, managing the employees, and retaining the employees is known as:

(A) Return of investment

(B) Compensation and benefits

(C) Contingent worker

(D) Human capital strategy

84. When an individual or parties invest financially in a business as a means to help cover the start-up capital needed for a new business venture, this is known as:

(A) Sole proprietorship

(B) Limited liability partnership

(C) Corporate investment

(D) Equity partnership

85. A business that is thinking on a global scale is an example of:

(A) Grievance

(B) Achievement

(C) Globalization

(D) Underappreciation

86. The process for filing a formal complaint against a coworker is known as:

(A) Employment procedure

(B) Grievance procedure

(C) Termination procedure

(D) Violation procedure

87. The ability of a business to employ individuals who are knowledgeable and talented is known as:

(A) Human capital strategy

(B) Chain of command

(C) Sales and purchases

(D) Strategic planning

88. Professional relationships between staff members and managers are referred to as:

(A) Mechanical relations

(B) Industrial relations

(C) Socioeconomic relations

(D) Industry-leading standards

89. A way of measuring profits by calculating what has been earned in previous years in order to develop an estimated average for profits that will be gained in the future is known as:

(A) Return on investment

(B) Personal stakeholder

(C) Internal rate of return

(D) Perceived success

90. A private computer network that operates through the internet but is secure and grants limited access only to certain individuals is known as:

(A) Internet

(B) Proprietary software

(C) Private server

(D) Intranet

91. A group that is organized to obtain better wages, benefits, compensation, and working conditions is known as:

(A) Human resources

(B) Labor union

(C) Better Business Bureau

(D) Labor laws

92. A software system that is designed to take some of the workload off HR by tracking employee training and continued development is known as:

(A) Educational learning portal

(B) Closed network program

(C) Blended learning classroom

(D) Learning management system

93. An insurance policy that protects individuals, businesses and organizations in the event that an employee is kidnapped and held for ransom is known as:

(A) Life insurance policy

(B) Homeowner's insurance policy

(C) Business owner insurance policy

(D) Kidnap-and-ransom insurance policy

94. When an organization invests in its members of management, this is known as:

(A) Employee training

(B) Leadership promotion training

(C) Employee orientation

(D) Leadership development

95. A legal document that shows an individual's or business' rights to produce, sell, use, or otherwise utilize services that belong to an individual or entity under a copyright, trademark, or intellectual property is known as:

(A) Certificate

(B) Qualification

(C) License

(D) Endearment

96. A physical or virtual forum to conduct business is known as:

(A) Marketplace

(B) Database

(C) E-commerce

(D) Enterprise

97. When two or more businesses join in a business venture, this is known as:

(A) Acquisition

(B) Coup

(C) Merger

(D) Buyout

98. An outline of what a business wants to achieve and its overall purpose is known as:

(A) Mission statement

(B) Organizational development

(C) Moral absolute

(D) Philosophical goal

99. An employee who works with multiple companies at the same time is considered to be:

(A) Working overtime

(B) Moonlighting

(C) Opportunity-seeking

(D) Retiring

100. The skills, knowledge, and experience that an employee gains while working in a position are known as:

(A) On-the-job experience

(B) Training

(C) Further career development

(D) Specialized training

Test 2 Answers

1. (B) Upfront costs

   The upfront costs of any start-up include cash not made up of any assets or investments that are not liquidated.

2. (D) Securing capital for start-ups

   The HR department is responsible for many things, but securing financial start-up capital is not one of these things.

3. © Time to fill

   Time to fill refers to the amount of time from the moment a position becomes vacant until the time that same position is filled.

4. ©(C) Administrative duties

   Administrative duties are the responsibility of HR personnel. They include keeping detailed records, organizing and retaining information, and ensuring the security of all confidential documents.

5. (B) Tax equalization policy

   The tax equalization policy applies to employees who are from one country and are employed to work in another. This policy allows a portion of the individual's taxes to be paid to the person's native country and the other portion to be paid to the country in which the individual is employed. The setup for this policy is designed so that individuals pay a fair tax by splitting tax payments between the two countries rather than paying a higher tax to one single country alone.

6. (D) Stakeholders

   A stakeholder is an individual or entity that has a financial interest in an organization. The financial interest can be direct or indirect. Stakeholders may include employees, investors, suppliers, or owners, among others.

7. (D) Timeless

   S.M.A.R.T. stands for specific, measurable, action-oriented, realistic and time-based goals. Timelessness is not part of the S.M.A.R.T. system.

8. (A) Screening tools

   Screening tools are a way of assessing employees to determine if they are well suited for specific positions in a business.

9. ©(C) Restricted stock

   Restricted stock refers to an employee's inability to offload stocks or limitations placed on when they can sell stocks or shares.

10. (D) Reimbursements

    Reimbursements are the act of repaying funds that were previously borrowed or loaned to a person, group, entity, business, or organization for work, employment, or investment purposes.

11. ©(C) Qualifications

    Qualifications refers to a specific set of skills, abilities, and knowledge a prospective employee must have in order to qualify for a position in an organization.

12. (A) Organizational development

Organizational development involves assisting in planning, implementing, and organizing a business' plan©

13. (C) Moral absolute

    A moral absolute is when there is a clear line that defines right from wrong. There are no gray areas in a moral absolute.

14. (D) The employee is willing to relocate nationally or internationally for work.

    Mobility refers to an employee who is willing to relocate for a job, whether nationally or internationally.

15. (B) Merit increase

    A merit increase is a pay raise that is given to an employee for meeting job performance goals.

16. (B) Market salary survey

    A market salary survey is research conducted by a business in order to compare similar jobs in the employment market to determine what the average fair pay for a position is.

17. (A) Lump sum compensation

    Lump sum compensation is when the full value of a debt is paid all at the same time rather than in installments.

18. (B) A learning effectiveness model

    The ultimate goal of the learning effectiveness model is to make sure that a business' training and development programs are working effectively to help the company reach both its long-term and short-term goals. Any inefficiencies are highlighted by the model so they can then be addressed.

19. (C) Labor union

    A labor union is composed of a group of employees who are seeking fair wages, employer benefits, compensation, improved workplace conditions, or other similar employment-related necessities.

20. (A) Intranet

The intranet is a private computer network that operates through the internet but is secure and grants select individuals limited access to the information contained on that private network. An example of using an intranet would be a major company that has satellite offices in Madrid and a home office in New York. The company places the data on a private intranet network so that the work that one individual does during the day in Madrid can be reviewed by employees the same day in New York.

21. (A) Leadership development

Leadership development happens when a business invests in its own members of management or other leaders in the organization for the benefit not just of management but of the company as a whole.

22. (B) Joint venture

A joint venture is a business partnership created when two or more parties join to share in any financial failures or successes the joint vent© has.

23. (C) An individual who agrees to work outside his/her native country

An international assignee is an employee who agrees to work outside his/her native country.

24. (C) Insourcing

Insourcing is when individuals or groups in a business are repurposed to do a different job for their employer for a given project or period of time. Insourcing is usually done in order to save money.

25. (C) Incentives

Incentives are any rewards given to employees to motivate them. An example is an employer who offers a vacation to Hawaii to the individual or team that brings in the most sales for a given quarter.

26. (D) Hardship premium

When an employee suffers a particular hardship due to living in a difficult or dangerous place where a company is located, that employee may be paid an additional amount to compensate for the inconvenience.

27. (D) When a business builds all new facilities on newly purchased land.

A greenfield operation refers to a business venture that is brand-new and is just being started from the ground up.

28. (C) Employment at will

Employment at will is defined as the working relationship that employers have with their ©ff or employees.

29. (C) Environmental responsibility

Environmental responsibility refers to an organization's responsibilities to the environment, employees, and the communities in which a business is located. These responsibilities include ensuring that the way business is conducted is safe and healthy for all concerned. This includes disposing of toxic waste safely, recycling, etc.

30. (D) Employee relations

Employee relations are one of the key points of any business. Ensuring that employees can resolve conflicts, comply with regulations, understand and follow policies, are informed of their career development options, feel heard and respected by management, and can otherwise communicate in regards to the chain of command is incredibly important. Successful businesses thrive on positive employer-employee communication and relationships.

31. (B) Employee self-service

Employee self-service refers to the HR department allowing its staff members or employees to log into personal accounts that contain their employment information in order to manage and update their personal information. This information can include but is not limited to things such as home address, phone number, email address, emergency contacts, basic medical information, spouse, etc. A business allowing its staff members to update this information on their own takes some of the workload off HR personnel.

32. (A) Downsizing

Downsizing happens when a business reduces the number of employees it has for reasons such as streamlining production processes, creating a more efficient workflow, reducing employment redundancies, etc. Ultimately, downsizing is about generating profit, cutting waste, and being as efficient as possible.

33. (B) E-learning

E-learning allows employees a flexible way of completing training. E-learning does not require an instructor or in-class instruction but rather has checks and balances in place to track an employee's progress through the e-learning training program and to alert appropriate members of management when the program is complete.

34. (C) Dedicated HR personnel

Dedicated HR personnel are individuals who are hired to work only in the HR department in a company. Those individuals do not cross-train or otherwise work in any other area or department of that organization.

35. (A) A defined benefits plan

A defined benefits plan is a retirement or pension plan that allows for payments to be made at regular intervals to the retiree upon their retirement. Commonly, retirement payments on this sort of benefits plan are made biweekly, monthly, semiannually, or annually.

36. (C) Credentials

Credentials are a form of certification that physically shows an employment applicant or employee possesses a specific skill set, knowledge base, or ability. It is common for an organization to verify employment applicants' credentials to ensure that they meet the minimum requirements for a job prior to being hired.

37. (C) Cross-training

Cross-training is when an employee who works in one particular job is additionally trained to do one or more jobs in the organization. An example of cross-training might be an employee who works in housekeeping being cross-trained to run the front desk. Cross-training helps ensure that if a business is understaffed, an employee is out sick, or a position is otherwise vacant, someone in the company is available to capably do the job. Cross-training can eliminate the need for outside employment assistance or temp services, or it can simply help reduce redundancies in a business.

38. (B) Corporate citizenship

Corporate citizenship refers to corporations reaching out to assist the local communities in which they are located.

39. (C) Corporate social responsibility

Corporate social responsibility is the commitment a company makes to its local community in order to better the environment and the community as a whole for housing the company.

40. (C) Certification

Certification is an electronic or paper credential that shows that an individual, business, or organization has undergone a certain training course, completed a program, possesses a certain set of skills, etc.

41. (A) Cloud computing

Cloud computing is a method businesses utilize in order to keep their information secure on a server while also still using the internet to share that information with other parties as needed.

42. (C) Compliance

For a business to be in compliance, it must follow company policies and procedures, as well as local, state, and federal laws. It also must meet legal, health, safety, and economic standards.

43. (D) Accepting benefits and compensation when offered

Career planning revolves around setting professional goals, analyzing how to reach those goals, and taking the steps to meet each goal in a timely and efficient manner.

44. (A) Revenue sources

A breakdown analysis uses a business' revenue, sources of revenue, and other key points to assess a business' success.

45. (A) Buy-in

A buy-in involves investing money in a business. The partnership that is created through the buy-in can be either a permanent investment or a temporary investment once paid back in full, with any interest or contractual duties included.

46. (C) Beneficiary

A beneficiary is a person or entity that is given the benefits of a plan or policy. This usually refers to the financial benefits from a final will, life insurance policy, or retirement plan.

47. (B) Best practices

Best practices are a way of helping a business produce long-term results and achieve organizational goals.

48. (C) Application tracking system

An application tracking system is designed to help the HR department, team leaders, business owners, or anyone else involved with the recruiting and hiring of employees keep applicants' information secure and organized.

49. (A) Background checks

Businesses often do detailed background checks on potential employees. Some organizations even go so far as to conduct additional background checks before promoting from within. Background checks can be personal, professional, financial, or criminal. These checks are done to ensure that the candidates being placed in these positions have the abilities required to do the job and do not have any red flags that might mean they could harm the company.

50. (D) Appeal

An appeal is an official method that can be used to challenge legal findings or conclusions.

51. (B) Apprentice

An apprentice is an individual who studies under an experienced professional in the same line of work. The experienced individual helps the apprentice learn the job. Apprentices are most often found in careers such as plumbing, carpentry, mechanics, and construction.

52. (A) Alternative dispute resolution

An alternative dispute resolution is a way to resolve a disagreement between parties in a business setting. It allows the parties involved to settle the disagreement without having to go through legal proceedings or file formal complaints or charges.

53. (C) Affirmative action

Affirmative action is when employers or HR personnel treat employment applicants in a way that levels the playing field during the application process.

54. (D) Accrual

Accrual is a method of accounting that highlights a business' financials by reviewing its income and expenses. This information is organized to compare paid invoices to receipts.

55. (B) The National Labor Relations Board

The National Labor Relations Board is responsible for enforcing labor laws in the United States.

56. (D) The Securities and Exchange Commission

The United States Securities and Exchange Commission is a federal organization that is responsible for protecting investors and maintaining orderly stock markets.

57. (A) The Worker Adjustment and Retraining Notification Act

Under this act, any factory or plant that has advance notice of any kind of serious layoffs or facility or plant closings is required by law to give its employees and its community a minimum of a 60 days' notice prior to when the layoffs will occur or the facility will close.

58. (D) The Department of Labor

The United States Department of Labor is responsible for maintaining minimum wage standards and oversees unemployment insurance, reemployment services, and occupational safety within the workplace.

59. (A) Elective abortions

Under the Pregnancy Discrimination Act, women who are already pregnant, become pregnant, or develop a health-related condition due to their pregnancy are granted protection under this law. However, if a woman has an elective abortion and develops any health-related complications due to the procedure, she is granted no protections.

60. (B) United States military service members

The Uniformed Services Employment and Reemployment Rights Act ensures that an employer cannot penalize employees for time that they are required to take away from their civilian jobs to serve in their military positions, including training and deployments. Furthermore, their job is protected while they are away serving their country. Upon the service members' return, employers are required to reinstate them to the position they had when they left, and they must receive any benefits due to them in their absence.

61. (B) Occupational Safety and Health Act

The Occupational Safety and Health Administration is responsible for limiting hazards in the workplace. It is able to do this under the Occupational Safety and Health Act, which allows OSHA to limit or eliminate toxic chemicals, dangerous noise levels, dangers related to machinery, exposure to excessive temperatures, and unsanitary working conditions. In the event that these conditions cannot be completely avoided, OSHA makes provisions to help protect individuals who will be exposed to such hazards.

62. (C) Expanding health-care coverage through public and private insurers, as well as expanding Medicare and Medicaid

Under the Patient Protection and Affordable Care Act, coverage was expanded for both public and private health insurance companies. Additionally, Medicaid and Medicare were expanded to provide more coverage and qualify more individuals for state-assisted insurance, particularly individuals who are low-income, disabled, and elderly.

63. (B) Immigration laws as they pertain to employment

The Immigration and Nationality Act applies to all immigration-related issues as they pertain to employment in the United States. It protects employment candidates and employees from being discriminated against based on their immigration status. It also assists those seeking temporary or permanent employment in the United States who are not naturalized citizens. The act also requires employers to verify the employment eligibility of candidates by having them complete the federal I-9 form as part of the hiring process.

64. (C) Immigration and Nationality Act

The Immigration and Nationality Act helps prevent employers from providing unsafe work environments, paying less than minimum wage, or otherwise discriminating against employees based on immigration status or their legal right to work in the United States.

65. (B) Fitness workouts at employer facilities

Federal labor laws protect employees and ensure that they receive payment when doing work-related activities. Employees are guaranteed to be paid when completing orientation, training or receiving continued education for their employers, and during rest periods and business-related meals. However, while having the privilege of working out at a facility may be a perk a company offers, such a benefit is not required of employers.

66. (A) A genetic predisposition to an illness

Under the Genetic Information Nondiscrimination Act, employers are not allowed to discriminate against employment candidates or employees because of a predisposition to possibly developing an illness later on.

67. (B) Equal Pay Act

Under the Equal Pay Act, men and women may not be discriminated against in regard to their wages if the individuals possess the same qualifications and work in the same field, and the work requires the same working conditions and same efforts.

68. (C) The United States Family and Medical Leave Act

Privately owned employers who have more than 50 employees who work more than 20 workweeks in the current or preceding calendar year are bound by this law. Public agencies, such as primary and secondary schools, local government, state government, and federal government agencies, are also bound by this law regardless of how many employees they have.

69. (A) The Securities and Exchange Commission

It is the job of the United States Securities and Exchange Commission to protect investors, ensure fairness in the industry, maintain the order and efficiency of the market, and help form capital.

70. (D) All of the above

The Dodd-Frank Wall Street Reform and Consumer Protection Act was created to ensure that taxpayer dollars are not used to bail out publicly traded companies, make publicly traded companies accountable for their actions, ensure that publicly traded companies are transparent about their finances with the general public, and create financial stability within those environments.

71. (B) More than 15 employees

According to federal law, any employer with 15 or more employees is bound by the Civil Rights Act of 1964. Those employers cannot discriminate against employment candidates or employees as pertains to being hired, fired, or promoted, transitioning to another job, or seeking additional job training, continued education, or other similarly related employment advancements.

72. (A) COBRA

The Consolidated Omnibus Budget Reconciliation Act is most commonly known as COBRA. Most often, employee handbooks and HR department professionals will refer to it as COBRA insurance.

73. (B) The Americans with Disabilities Act

The Americans with Disabilities Act was enacted to prevent employers from discriminating against potential employment candidates and employees due to a physical or mental disability. The ADA is a federally regulated law and in some cases is additionally supported by state and local laws as well. It also prevents discrimination in regard to employees seeking promotions or transferring to other positions. ADA requires employers to make reasonable accommodations to allow disabled individuals to do their job effectively.

74. (D) Americans with Disabilities rights

Employers who have one or more employees with a disability are required by federal law, and in some cases additionally required by state laws, to post an Americans with Disabilities poster listing employee rights and responsibilities. Federally regulated employment posters should be placed in locations that employees frequent. Such locations include break rooms and employee locker rooms.

75. (D) Interview

During the interview process, there are usually at least two rounds of interviews. Interviewing individuals helps HR representatives understand a candidate's past employment and assess their qualifications and knowledge. The interviewing process is an important step in ensuring that a qualified candidate not only possesses the skills and abilities needed to do the job but also will mesh well with the work environment.

76. (C) Anywhere internationally

The aPHR is an internationally accredited certification gained by completing an exam and earning certification. Once gained, the aPHR certification credentials can be used throughout the world.

77. (C) Overall business success

From screening employees and hiring qualified candidates, to ensuring proper training and development, facilitating employer-employee relations, and managing the health and safety of an organization, HR's tasks are all geared toward ensuring a business' overall success.

78. (A) Minimum wage

The lowest amount of money that a business can legally pay an employee is known as minimum wage. There is a federal minimum wage law. Some states choose to take it one step further and have their own minimum wage laws that are slightly higher than the minimum wage set by the United States federal government.

79. (C) Job database

A job database is an accounting of all of the employment positions in an organization. Using a spreadsheet, computer program, or software system, a business will list all the employment positions in the organization. Then, a detailed list of what each job entails will be outlined. Finally, the abilities, knowledge, and skills an individual will need to possess in order to adequately fill a position will be listed. That database is used as a reference point any time a position needs to be filled and can be updated as a business grows and changes.

80. (D) The Bureau of Labor Statistics

The Bureau of Labor Statistics is responsible for collecting information on a continual basis to keep an up-to-date record of job outlooks in the United States. The information collected includes the Bureau of Labor Statistics' Occupational Outlook Handbook. This handbook includes projected job growth in the United States based on up-to-date statistics.

81. (B) Business structures

A sole proprietorship, limited liability partnership, limited liability company, and corporation are all types of business structures. A business structure entails the way an organization is set up, who is responsible for its operation, who is liable for any negative impacts to the business, who takes a loss if the organization does not do well, and who reaps the rewards when the business succeeds.

82. (B) Compliance

Keeping an organization, business, or partnership in compliance is an important part of HR's responsibilities. Compliance helps ensure that a business is doing things legally, prevent lawsuits or liabilities, and set standards for the company in the long term.

83. (D) Human capital strategy

The human capital strategy is a standardized method used in businesses to accomplish three employment tasks: recruiting, retention, and workforce planning.

84. (D) Equity partnership

An equity partnership is a business structure in which two or more parties invest financially in a business. This investment is made as part of a business venture to generate start-up capital.

85. (C) Globalization

Globalization involves thinking on an international scale, rather than just a national one, in terms of business practices.

86. (B) Grievance procedure

A grievance procedure is the process that an organization puts into place as a means of addressing any workplace problems. The exact way a grievance is handled depends on the issue.

87. (A) Human capital strategy

Human capital strategy is the ability of an organization or business to recruit and retain knowledgeable and talented staff members.

88. (B) Industrial relations

The term *industrial relations* refers to the members of management in the industrial field and their professional business relationships with staff. Specifically, it sets guidelines, regulations, and laws that pertain to how those relationships can legally be conducted.

89. (C) Internal rate of return

The internal rate of return is a method for measuring profits and estimating potential future profits. For example, if Anna has earned $100,000 every year for the past four years between November 1 and December 3, it can logically be assumed that she will earn a similar amount in the future.

90. (D) Intranet

An intranet is a private online computer network that grants limited access to those who are allowed to see the information contained on that network. For example, many large corporations use an intranet to share confidential information with certain parties.

91. (B) Labor union

A labor union refers to employees who unite with the common goal of improving wages, benefits, compensation, or working conditions by coming to a reasonable agreement between employees and employer.

92. (D) Learning management system

Learning management systems are software systems that lessen some of the work of HR personnel. Such software is designed to track new and existing employees, as well as their training and continued education, individual successes, areas of struggle, development opportunities, etc.

93. (D) Kidnap-and-ransom insurance policy

Individuals, organizations, businesses, and corporations working in high-risk areas may choose to have such insurance protection in the event that someone employed or associated with any of these entities is kidnapped and held for ransom.

94. (D) Leadership development

Leadership development is when a business invests in its members of management. Doing so allows members of management to become more effective and better equipped to do their jobs. Leadership development can also include preparing current employees for future positions or promotions.

95. (C) License

When an individual, entity, or organization owns a product, service, copyright, trademark, or intellectual property, an outside individual or entity must obtain a license in order to use that process, product, method, or intellectual property.

96. (A) Marketplace

A marketplace is the physical or virtual place in which businesses operate. This type of marketplace, much like a supermarket, allows multiple entities to come to the platform and sell their products and services.

97. (C) Merger

A merger occurs when two or more entities join in a business venture and create a new, shared, and legally binding entity. A merger also occurs when two or more businesses join to purchase another organization. The purchase ensures that the parties are bound legally and share their own overall joint resources.

98. (A) Mission statement

A mission statement is a written description or outline of a business' purpose. A mission statement remains consistent from the inception of that business until its conclusion.

99. (B) Moonlighting

An employee of one company working at another job(s) in his/her off-hours is considered to be moonlighting.

100. (A) On-the-job experience

On-the-job experience is when employees learn their position or trade, gain knowledge and skills, and otherwise learn the ropes of a job by physically doing it.

Test 3 (100 Questions)

1. What are the two factors that affect a business' performance?

   (A) Internal and external

   (B) Sales and marketing strategies

   (C) Income and expenses

   (D) Workforce and strategy

2. To keep a company in compliance means:

   (A) Making sure that the company is meeting the safety recommendations of its industry

   (B) Ensuring that a company is following federal, state, and local laws, as well as any rules or guidelines that should be met by company, industry, health, and safety standards

   (C) Making sure that all employees have filled out their health insurance information in a timely manner and before open enrollment ends for the year

   (D) Ensuring that all applicants turn in the appropriate information with their application, including applications, proper identification, and consent for a background check

3. Which United States organization compiles a list of most jobs and outlines the responsibilities each job entails?

   (A) The Bureau of Labor

   (B) OSHA

   (C) The Department of Labor

   (D) Workforce Services

4. The Family and Medical Leave Act applies to any organization that has more than how many employees?

(A) 50

(B) 1

(C) Any disabled employees

(D) 12

5. The process of attracting potential candidates for employment through advertising and job fairs is known as:

(A) Termination

(B) Development

(C) Hiring

(D) Recruitment

6. If the ___________ is/are too long and complicated, it/they will discourage recruitment efforts.

(A) Benefits package

(B) Application process

(C) Tax forms

(D) Retirement package

7. What does the acronym aPHR stand for?

(A) Applies Principles of Human Resources

(B) Associate Professional in Human Resources

(C) Associates in Professional and Human Reparations

(D) Authorized Personal Health Representative

8. Which of the following is the correct acronym for the Family and Medical Leave Act?

    (A) FMLA

    (B) HIPAA

    (C) OSHA

    (D) EPPA

9. Which of the following organizations is responsible for overseeing the United States' Fair Labor Standards Act?

    (A) The United States Department of Labor

    (B) The Department of Immigration and Nationality

    (C) The Occupational Safety and Health Administration

    (D) The Department of Homeland Security

10. Which of the following posters must be hung somewhere it is clearly visible to employees for any company that has a disabled employee?

    (A) The Family and Medical Leave Act poster

    (B) The Occupational Safety and Health Act poster

    (C) The Workers with Disabilities Act poster

    (D) The Fair Labor Standards Act poster

11. Hiring qualified individuals to work in a company is an important role of HR because:

    (A) Good employees help ensure the success of a business.

    (B) It ensures employees will not quit.

    (C) It ensures employees can handle confidential materials.

    (D) It ensures candidates will be approved for security clearance.

12. Organizations may offer health benefits, 401k plan options, PTO time, sick leave, vacation time, maternity leave, paternity leave, holiday pay, or other similar compensation as part of:

   (A) Pension plans

   (B) Benefits packages

   (C) Stock options

   (D) Severance packages

13. Which of the following laws prevents employees from being discriminated against if they are 40 years of age or older?

   (A) The Consolidated Budget Reconciliation Act

   (B) The Employee Retirement Income Security Act

   (C) The Age Discrimination in Employment Act

   (D) The Fair Labor Standards Act

14. Per __________, individuals cannot be discriminated against in regard to employment based on their race, color, religion, sex, or national origin.

   (A) The Civil Rights Act

   (B) The Pregnancy Discrimination Act

   (C) The Equal Pay Act

   (D) The Fair Labor Standards Act

15. In the event that employees take FMLA, they are given the opportunity to utilize COBRA, which means they are given:

    (A) The right to not be discriminated against because of pregnancy or a pregnancy-related condition

    (B) The right to not be discriminated against due to physical or mental disabilities

    (C) The right to work in a harassment-free environment in which people feel safe and are treated with respect

    (D) The right to keep their health-care insurance through their employer

16. Compensation practices must be followed by all publicly traded companies per ___________:

    (A) The Age Discrimination in Employment Act

    (B) The Dodd-Frank Wall Street Reform and Consumer Protection Act

    (C) The Civil Rights Act

    (D) The Employee Retirement Income Security Act

17. Any individuals who pay into a retirement or pension plan are guaranteed by the __________ that those funds will be there and will remain protected until their retirement.

    (A) Equal Pay Act

    (B) Age Discrimination in Employment Act

    (C) Employee Retirement Income Security Act

    (D) Occupational Safety and Health Act

18. Under the __________, the majority of employers are not allowed to require employment candidates or employees to take lie detector tests.

    (A) Fair Credit Reporting Act

    (B) Fair Labor Standards Act

    (C) Employment Polygraph Protection Act

    (D) National Labor Relations Act

19. In order to qualify for FMLA, employees must meet all of the following criteria except:

    (A) Employees must work for their employer for at least one year.

    (B) Employees must be full-time.

    (C) Employees must have worked at least 1,250 hours in the current 12-month time frame.

    (D) Employees must work for an employer who is located within 75 miles and has at least 50 employees.

20. If employers and their employees meet the criteria, they are guaranteed mandatory breaks under which law?

    (A) The Fair Labor Standards Act

    (B) The Equal Opportunity Employment Laws

    (C) The Occupational Safety and Health Act

    (D) The Health Insurance Portability and Accountability Act

21. Which of the following organizations regulates and enforces the Genetic Information Nondiscrimination Act?

    (A) The Equal Employment Opportunity Commission

    (B) The Department of Labor

    (C) The Division of Civil Rights

    (D) The Department of Civil Liberties

22. HIPAA was enacted in order to do what?

(A) To ensure employees have health insurance coverage

(B) To make sure that employees are able to retire with the benefits that they have put in during their career

(C) To ensure employees' privacy in regards to health insurance and health care

(D) To guarantee an employee who meets the criteria time off after having a child

23. The Occupational Safety and Health Act was developed in order to:

(A) Ensure that employees with disabilities can still be hired

(B) Regulate the health-care industry

(C) Ensure that women are not discriminated against due to childbirth or pregnancy-related health concerns

(D) Ensure the overall safety and health of employees in the workplace

24. Under OSHA regulations, an employer must provide all of the following except ___________ for employees.

(A) Ear protection when working in environments with excessive or hazardous noise levels

(B) Protective clothing covering when working in an environment that exposes them to hazardous chemicals or waste

(C) Hard hats when working in construction or other heavy machinery– related areas

(D) Personal protective equipment when working in an office environment

25. Under Obamacare previously, all individuals nationwide had to purchase:

(A) Life insurance

(B) Dental insurance

(C) Health insurance

(D) Homeowner's insurance

26. Under the ________, employers are forbidden from discriminating against employment candidates and employees based on pregnancy or pregnancy-related conditions.

(A) Pregnancy Discrimination Act

(B) Equal Opportunity Employment Act

(C) Civil Rights Act

(D) Uniformed Services Employment and Reemployment Rights Act

27. Per the ___________, military service members called to duty can return to their previous jobs without losing seniority or being penalized for their time gone.

(A) Equal Opportunity Employment Act

(B) Uniformed Services Employment and Reemployment Rights Act

(C) Worker Adjustment and Retraining Notification Act

(D) None of the above

28. The Worker Adjustment and Retraining Notification Act is implemented and overseen by:

(A) The Department of Human Services

(B) The International Labor Organization

(C) The Department of Labor

(D) The Employee Benefits Security Administration

29. The organization responsible for administering, regulating, and enforcing the terms that are protected under Title I of the Employment Retirement Income Securities Act is known as:

(A) The Equal Employment Opportunity Commission

(B) The Department of Labor

(C) The Employee Benefits Security Administration

(D) The International Labor Organization

30. The organization that is responsible for protecting federal merit systems in the workplace is known as:

(A) The Federal Trade Commission

(B) The International Labor Organization

(C) The Merit System Protection Board

(D) The National Labor Relations Board

31. Which organization is responsible for investigating any concerns as they apply to an individual's civil rights?

(A) The United States Commission on Civil Rights

(B) The Equal Employment Opportunity Commission

(C) The Department of Labor

(D) The Employee Benefits Security Administration

32. Which of the following United States organizations is responsible for programs developed to help military veterans continue their education or gain other skills required to enter or reenter the workforce following their service to their country?

(A) The United States Department of Veterans Affairs

(B) The Board of Veterans' Appeals

(C) The Veterans' Employment and Training Service

(D) The Veterans Benefits Administration

33. The purchase of a business is most often referred to in legal terms as a/an:

(A) Acquisition

(B) Merger

(C) Take over

(D) Monopoly

34. When a business finds an impromptu solution to an issue, this is known as:

(A) Nickel and dime

(B) Resolution

(C) Strategizing

(D) Ad hoc

35. An agreement between two parties that creates a partnership that is mutually beneficial is known as:

(A) Disunity

(B) Alliance

(C) Enmity

(D) Severance

36. A method that is utilized to standardize exam scores is known as:

(A) Angoff

(B) SAGE

(C) Z score

(D) Central tendency

37. A legal proceeding that allows parties to go before a judge in order to have a speedy ruling made in return for not being able to overturn or appeal that decision is known as:

(A) Mediation

(B) Arbitration

(C) Summarization

(D) Directed verdict

38. A training method that uses online learning as a resource for educational professionals and instructors in order for them to work with students and employees in different time zones is known as:

(A) Distance learning

(B) Blended learning

(C) Asynchronous learning

(D) E-learning

39. A business model that standardizes salaries, benefits, and compensation for positions in a business is known as:

(A) Benefits package

(B) Benefits program

(C) Checks and balances

(D) Balance sheet

40. An interviewing technique that uses employees' past employment history to help determine their future employment performance is known as:

(A) Behavioral interview

(B) Personality analysis

(C) Reference review

(D) Interpersonal skills test

41. Educational background and employment history is which type of data?

(A) Employment data

(B) Biographical data

(C) Financial data

(D) Investment data

42. When a mix of in-classroom and e-learning is used for training, this is known as:

(A) Blended learning

(B) E-learning

(C) Virtual learning

(D) Standard learning

43. The process of growing and developing one's career is known as:

(A) Career management

(B) Career plateau

(C) Career development

(D) Career stagnancy

44. The process of planning and pursuing one's professional goals is known as:

(A) Social climbing

(B) Career management

(C) Chain of command

(D) Hiring within

45. A set of international ethical guidelines for organizations is known as:

(A) International Labor Commission

(B) Caux Principles

(C) Environmental Ethical Principles and Responsibilities

(D) United Nations Environment Program

46. The process of combining resources, streamlining work for efficiency, cutting down on unnecessary waste of resources, and otherwise making a business function at a more efficient level with less redundancy and waste is an example of:

(A) Expansion

(B) Condensation

(C) Consolidation

(D) Merger

47. When a company hires an outside entity to do part or all of its production for a specific project, this is known as:

(A) Insourcing

(B) Outsourcing

(C) Contract manufacturing

(D) Subcontractor

48. What tool can be used to analyze the costs of a business start-up, the cost of running the business, and the prospective earnings it will generate in the future?

(A) Start-up cost analysis

(B) Benefits and compensation analysis

(C) Debt-to-profit analysis

(D) Cost-benefits analysis

49. What recruiting tool measures the costs of advertising, recruiting, paying employees, and training them?

(A) Cost per hire

(B) Annual percentage rate

(C) Cost of living adjustment

(D) Merit raise

50. A training technique that organizations utilize, especially those that conduct business internationally, with other organizations that have different cultures is known as:

(A) Cultural coaching

(B) Employee relations

(C) Political training

(D) Best practices

51. The amount of time that it takes for the HR department to fill a vacant position in a business is known as:

(A) Open enrollment

(B) Days to fill

(C) Minimum criterion

(D) Days on the market

52. A training method that employers use where all learning is done in a remote way using TV, DVDs, computers, and online streaming is known as:

(A) Distributed training

(B) E-learning

(C) Distance learning

(D) Flex schedule training

53. The amount of time the HR personnel of an organization are required to keep specific documents is known as:

(A) Compliance

(B) Regulations

(C) Validation

(D) Retention

54. A program that some organizations use that assists employees with personal issues outside work in order to make sure that those personal issues do not affect an individual's work performance is known as:

(A) Employee assistance program

(B) Compensation and benefits program

(C) Personal and family leave program

(D) Employee training program

55. A written set of information that may include an organization's benefits programs, codes of conduct, compensation, policies, and procedures is known as:

(A) Employment contract

(B) Employee handbooks or manuals

(C) HR manuals

(D) Benefits packages

56. The frequency with which employees leave a business or with which a business experiences unfilled positions is known as:

(A) Employee retention

(B) Contracted employment

(C) Employee turnover

(D) Employee partnerships

57. Benefits that a business provides to employees or staff and that the company absorbs the cost of are known as:

(A) Employer branding

(B) Employee-paid benefits

(C) COBRA insurance

(D) Employer-paid benefits

58. When an organization has a set of beliefs and a defined idea of what appropriate behaviors are, these ideas are known as:

(A)An organization's vision

(B)A business' company culture

(C)A corporation's mission statement

(D)An organization's theme statement

59. A clear idea of what a business wants in the future that is put into writing for all to see is known as:

    (A) A company motto

    (B) A mission statement

    (C) Company culture

    (D) Defined values

60. A written statement that gives a brief description of a business' intents is known as:

    (A) Vision statement

    (B) Company culture

    (C) A value statement

    (D) Personal preference

61. Paperwork disclosing a business' policies, procedures, conduct, and various other topics related to employment is known as:

    (A) Employment contract

    (B) Employee handbook

    (C) Severance package

    (D) Operations manual

62. Of the following, ___________ would most likely require a full HR department.

(A)A single mom working as a real estate agent for her own personal small business

(B)A large corporation with satellite offices in England, Italy ,and Germany

(C)A sole proprietor of a small auto mechanic shop on the outskirts of a small town, with one other employee

(D)Two friends who are equal partners in a small contracting company

63. A company is in its start-up phase. There are currently three department managers. Anna is the new manager of HR. Today she is meeting with each of the department managers to discuss the job positions that need to be filled in the company. The list of positions, the comprehensive description of the jobs available, and a list of minimum job qualifications are used for:

(A) Job vacancy

(B) Recruitment

(C) Job database

(D) Job analysis

64. Olivia, who is wheelchair-bound but otherwise healthy and capable, applies for a position with a company. The position will require her to sit at a desk, answer phones, and work on the computer. The company uses floor-to-ceiling-height filing cabinets in each employee's cubicle. Olivia requests three waist-high filing cabinets. The cost to the company is minimal, and the shorter filing cabinets will conveniently fit in the workspace she has been assigned. This type of accommodation is known as:

(A) Reasonable accommodations

(B) Unrealistic expectations

(C) Employment compensations

(D) Undue hardships

65. Eleanor is 60 years old. She just graduated from college with her bachelor's degree in computer science and administration. Eleanor applies for a job at a local company. She meets all of the requirements to be hired for the job, and as it turns out, she is the best candidate from all of those that applied. However, the HR manager feels that Eleanor is too old for the job. This is what kind of discrimination?

(A) Gender discrimination

(B) Racial discrimination

(C) Age discrimination

(D) Ethical discrimination

66. Tracking how employees are progressing in their job is an important part of:

(A) Performance

(B) Management

(C) Operations

(D) Mediation

67. The individuals who manage a group of employees but are below a department manager are known as:

(A) Staff units

(B) Team leaders

(C) Line management

(D) Focus groups

68. When behavioral sciences are combined with business as a means of analyzing and improving the way a business operates as a whole, this is known as:

(A) Compensatory training

(B) Distributive techniques

(C) Organizational development

(D) Delphine technique

69. Which of the following laws was amended in 2008 to ensure broader coverage for individuals with disabilities in the workplace?

(A) Civil Rights Act

(B) Americans with Disabilities Act Amendments Act

(C) Sarbanes-Oxley Act

(D) Americans with Disabilities Act

70. If a company is downsizing, which of the following is most likely to occur?

(A) Hiring

(B) Promotions

(C) Incentives

(D) Layoffs

71. An organization's mission, business goals, and objectives fall under which of the following categories?

(A) Workforce planning

(B) Employee and labor relations

(C) Business management and strategies

(D) Risk management

72. Unethical behavior is defined under which of the following laws?

(A) The Clayton Antitrust Act

(B) The Labor Management Reporting and Disclosure Act

(C) The Patent Act

(D) The Service Contract Act

73. Which of the following laws outlawed monopolies?

(A) The Clayton Antitrust Act

(B) The Longshore and Harbor Workers' Compensation Act

(C) The Public Contract Act

(D) The Sherman Antitrust Act

74. Which act establishes a board and raises money for unemployment compensation and benefits the general welfare of individuals who are senior citizens, are disabled, have children with disabilities, or have other dependents?

(A) The Social Security Act

(B) The Federal Insurance Contributions Act

(C) The Federal Unemployment Tax Act

(D) The Public Contract Act

75. Which act ensures that temporary employees will get fringe benefits once they have worked on a project that is worth more than $2500?

(A) The Equal Pay Act

(B) The Workers' Compensation Act

(C) The Portal-to-Portal Act

(D) The Service Contract Act

76. Which of the following laws was enacted to protect consumers by requiring lenders to state the terms and conditions of all loans in a way that is easily understood?

(A) The Service Contract Act

(B) The Consumer Credit Protection Act

(C) The Federal Insurance Contributions Act

(D) The Clayton Antitrust Act

77. Facilitating the relationship between employers and employees is part of:

(A) Risk management

(B) Compensation and benefits

(C) Employee relations

(D) Loss prevention

78. The federal law that mandates that employers withhold the correct amount from employees' pay for the purpose of paying into Medicare and Social Security is:

(A) The Health and Insurance Protection Act

(B) The Social Security Act

(C) The Federal Insurance Contributions Act

(D) The Service Contract Act

79. The policies in place to ensure the safest work environment possible and handle events that occur from the fallout of work-related injuries or illness related to employment are part of:

(A) Risk management

(B) Business management and strategy

(C) Workforce planning and environment

(D) Employee and labor relations

80. What federal law allows the United States government to tax businesses that have employees in order for the states to generate revenue for unemployment benefits?

(A) The Federal Employment Compensation Act

(B) The Labor Management Reporting and Disclosure Act

(C) The Federal Insurance Contributions Act

(D) The Federal Unemployment Tax Act

81. The law that grants rights to unions and union members is:

(A) The Social Security Act

(B) The Labor Management Reporting and Disclosure Act

(C) The Consumer Credit Protection Act

(D) The Portal-to-Portal Act

82. Which federal law provides medical care, rehabilitation, and wage compensation to anyone who is injured or disabled while navigating United States' waters or harbors or otherwise working where such vessels are being loaded, unloaded, built, or repaired?

(A) The Railway Labor Act

(B) The Social Security Act

(C) The Longshore and Harbor Workers' Compensation Act

(D) The Labor Management Reporting and Disclosure Act

83. Which law protects inventions from being made, used, or sold by others without express written permission?

(A) The Civil Rights Act

(B) The Public Contract Act

(C) The Patent Act

(D) The Public Safety Act

84. Employee rights, workplace behavior, unfair labor practices, positive employee relations, and employee termination procedures are all part of:

(A) Risk management

(B) Compensation and benefits

(C) Human resources development

(D) Employee and labor relations

85. Which law requires an employer to pay employees for their time spent working on the actual job and does not include travel time?

(A) The Portal-to-Portal Act

(B) The Equal Pay Act

(C) The Equal Opportunity Employment Act

(D) The Public Contract Act

86. What does the Clayton Antitrust Act do?

(A) It clearly defines what the minimum wage and maximum hours are under United States federal law.

(B) It clearly defines what unethical behavior is under United States federal law.

(C) It clearly defines what a trust is under United States federal law and how it can be used or applied.

(D) It clearly defines what ethical behavior is under United States federal law.

87. Under which law are contract standards set for those hired to work a contracted job over $15,000?

(A) The Equal Employment Opportunities Act

(B) The Fair Wages Act

(C) The Public Contract Act

(D) The Service Contract Act

88. Which law protects the airline industry?

(A) The Railway Labor Act

(B) The Fair Labor Act

(C) The Equal Pay Act

(D) The Public Contract Act

89. Why is performing an analysis on all jobs in a company and compiling a job database important?

(A) To know what jobs are vacant in a business

(B) To create a baseline for wage range throughout the company.

(C) To have current information on the jobs in a business and what is required to fill them if they become vacant

(D) To know which jobs have already been filled and which are left to be filled in a business

90. Which of the following documents is required when completing employment paperwork?

(A) W-4 form

(B) Application

(C) I-9 form

(D) W-2 form

91. An employee may quit at any time and an employer may terminate an employee at any time under which of the following laws?

(A) Respondent superior

(B) Implied contract

(C) Employment at will

(D) Employment relationship

92. When a local steel mill plant lays off 640 employees, what law affords the employees and their community some protections?

(A) The Workforce Adjustment and Retraining Act

(B) The Health Insurance Portability and Accountabilities Act

(C) The Consolidated Omnibus Budget Reconciliation Act

(D) The Equal Opportunity Employment Act

93. Which of the following formats makes the application process easier and therefore attracts more applicants?

(A) Paper application

(B) Mobile device application

(C) Online application

(D) None of the above

94. The Age Discrimination in Employment Act provides protection for people aged ________.

(A) Under 60

(B) 40 and over

(C) Under 18

(D) Under 40

95. Which of the following do small businesses choose to do rather than employ their own fully functioning HR department?

(A) Insource

(B) Hire

(C) Merge

(D) Outsource

96. If Hector is hired for a job and, in order to teach him how to do the job, his supervisor takes him out to the floor and teaches him right on the line, this type of training is known as:

(A) Hands-on learning

(B) Blended learning

(C) Virtual learning

(D) E-learning

97. Earning a merit raise means people earn a raise ____________.

(A) Based on how long they have been with a business

(B) Based on the amount of work they have put in and how well they have done their job

(C) Based on the commissions they have earned

(D) None of the above.

98. If an individual takes a job in a war zone, the employer should provide ________.

(A) Hazard pay

(B) A merit raise

(C) An assignment bonus

(D) A seniority raise

99. If an employee is harmed while on the job, the person is entitled to:

(A) Unemployment insurance

(B) Workers' compensation

(C) COBRA

(D) None of the above

100. Produce, develop, compensate, integrate, and maintain are the key functions of:

(A) Labor relations

(B) Corporate development

(C) Employment agencies

(D) HR

Test 3 Answers

1. (A) Internal and external

    Internal factors include the role that HR plays in a business, the mixture of skills that a business' workforce is made up of, the organizational culture, business strategy, and operations. External factors include the climate of the labor market, competition from other businesses, academic theories in use, and industry best practices. These factors affect a business' overall performance.

2. (B) Ensuring that a company is following the federal, state, and local laws, as well as any rules or guidelines that should be met by company, industry, health, and safety standards

    Part of HR's role is to ensure that an organization stays in compliance with the industry. Among other things, HR is responsible for ensuring that state and federal signage regarding employee rights is clearly posted, business and employee paperwork is kept up to date, files are retained for the appropriate amount of time, certifications and licensing are up to date, and the appropriate parties are informed when certifications and licensing are due for renewal.

3. (C) The Department of Labor

    The United States Department of Labor maintains a database that formally outlines almost every job in the United States. The information in the database includes a description of jobs by employers, the tasks and responsibilities required while working in a given job, any environmental implications a job may have, and any other important job-related information.

4. (A) 50

    Though there are a few exceptions, in general, any business that has 50 employees or more is bound by the Family and Medical Leave Act.

5. (D) Recruitment

Recruitment is an important responsibility of the HR department.

6. (B) Application process

   If the application process is too lengthy or complicated, then people are less likely to apply for a job. Being able to draw in qualified candidates is important for any business. In order to achieve this, many companies make applications available online and/or compatible with cell phones and tablets. They also streamline the application process to make it as easy as possible.

7. (B) Associate Professional in Human Resources

   aPHR stands for Associate Professional in Human Resources. This is an entry-level certification that is highly sought-after by employers hiring for the HR department.

8. (A) FMLA

   The Family and Medical Leave Act is better known as FMLA. Businesses with more than 50 employees are bound by the FMLA, and organizations must post visible FMLA federal signage in a location that employees frequent.

9. (A) The United States Department of Labor

   The United States Department of Labor is responsible for promoting work-related rights and benefits. The department helps oversee working conditions, helps advance or create opportunities for employment, and ensures that employees are receiving the benefits and rights they are entitled to by law.

10. (C) The Workers with Disabilities Act poster

    The Workers with Disabilities Act poster is a requirement for any employer who has one or more disabled employees. The sign must be placed in a location that is frequented by employees.

11. (A) Good employees help ensure the success of a business.

    For a business to succeed, it must employ qualified and knowledgeable employees who are capable of completing the tasks that are required of them.

12. (B) Benefits packages

    Many businesses offer some kind of benefits package. The most common benefit packages are offered to full-time employees, though some organizations also offer them to part-time employees. In the United States, the most common benefits packages include health benefits, dental benefits, 401k plans, PTO time or vacation time, sick leave, maternity leave, and holiday pay. Paternity leave is also becoming popular.

13. (C) The Age Discrimination in Employment Act

    This law federally mandates that an employer may not discriminate against applicants or employees who are 40 years old or older when it comes to hiring, moving up career ladders, wages, benefits, training, and layoffs.

14. (A) The Civil Rights Act

    According to federal law, an employer may not discriminate against an employment candidate or a current employee based on race, color, religion, sex, or national origin. Amendments to the act have been made to also include pregnancy, sexual orientation, and marital status.

15. (D) The right to keep their health-care insurance through their employer

    When employees take FMLA, they are given the opportunity to keep their health insurance through COBRA. COBRA insurance allows them to pay their premiums out of pocket while they are out of work temporarily for a set period of time.

16. (B) The Dodd-Frank Wall Street Reform and Consumer Protection Act

The Dodd-Frank Wall Street Reform and Consumer Protection Act was made law as a means of making publicly traded companies accountable for their actions, creating transparency and stopping the bailouts of publicly traded companies through the use of taxpayer dollars.

17. (C) Employee Retirement Income Security Act

Under this act, individuals who pay into a retirement plan or pension plan during their working lives are protected, and their money is protected so that they can receive the money that they have paid in when they retire.

18. (C) Employment Polygraph Protection Act

This act bans the majority of employers from using lie detector tests as part of the hiring process or in regard to hiring, firing, promoting, or performing other aspects of employment. Employers may not punish employees or discriminate against job candidates based on their refusal to take a polygraph.

19. (B) Employees must be full-time.

Under the FMLA, employees are not required to be full-time, but during the last 12 months, they must have worked a minimum of 1,250 hours.

20. (A) The Fair Labor Standards Act

This act, in addition to regulating child labor, also regulates required rest periods, work-related waiting periods, the requirements for work- or business-related meals, and legally mandated employee breaks.

21. (A) The Equal Employment Opportunity Commission

It is the responsibility of the EEOC to set the guidelines and enforce the law under the Genetic Information Nondiscrimination Act, which protects employees and employment candidates from being discriminated against by insurance providers and employers based on their predisposition to developing an illness.

22. (C) To ensure employees' privacy in regards to health insurance and health care

    Since many employers have access to their employees' health information, HIPAA helps to protect that information, ensures that employees cannot be discriminated against based on that information and protects that information from misuse.

23. (D) Ensure the overall safety and health of employees in the workplace

    The Occupational Safety and Health Act is a federally regulated law enforced through the Department of Labor. Under this law, the Occupational Safety and Health Administration is responsible for tracking and enforcing health and safety regulations in the workplace. It is especially critical for jobs that put employees into situations that could be hazardous or that require them to work with materials that could be hazardous.

24. (D) Personal protective equipment when working in an office environment

    The Occupational Safety and Health Administration is tasked with regulating and enforcing safety and health regulations in the workplace. This includes ensuring that employers provide employees with adequate personal protective equipment whenever it is necessary. Personal protective equipment can include but is not limited to safety glasses, hardhats, rubberized waterproof boots, clothing coverings, protective gloves, ear protection, and hazmat suits. OSHA sets the criteria for what type of PPE is required for each workplace environment.

25. (C) Health insurance

    Under the Patient Protection and Affordable Care Act, the United States used to require all individuals to purchase health insurance. Any individual who failed to purchase health insurance that met at least the minimum standards according to the law would have been subject to fines. This has now changed.

26. (A) Pregnancy Discrimination Act

While some states have their own laws, the Pregnancy Discrimination Act is a federal law that prevents employers from discriminating against job candidates and employees due to pregnancy or a pregnancy-related condition. Under the provisions of this law, women who are pregnant or become pregnant cannot be discriminated against, penalized, or fired. All employers who have at least 15 employees are held accountable to this law.

27. (B) Uniformed Services Employment and Reemployment Rights Act

All United States military personnel are granted protections for their civilian jobs, are prohibited from losing seniority, and cannot be penalized due to taking required time away from civilian jobs in order to fulfill their military commitments.

28. (C) The Department of Labor

The Department of Labor is responsible for enforcing the standard for minimum wage, unemployment insurance, reemployment services, and occupational safety, among others.

29. (C) The Employee Benefits Security Administration

The Employee Benefits Security Administration is responsible for administering, regulating and enforcing the terms that are covered under Title I of the Employee Retirement Income Security Act.

30. (C) The Merit System Protection Board

The Merit System Protection Board is tasked with protecting federal merit systems by preventing specific individuals from violating the systems through the abuse of power. It also protects United States federal employees.

31. (A) The United States Commission on Civil Rights

The United States Commission on Civil Rights is responsible for investigating, reporting, and recommending any concerns that are found in an organization as they pertain to individuals' civil rights and liberties.

32. (C) The Veterans' Employment and Training Service

The United States Veterans' Employment and Training Service is a program that is designed to help military veterans get the education that they require in order to enter or reenter the workforce after their military service.

33. (A) Acquisition

In its simplest terms, an acquisition is simply a business' purchase of a property from another individual, group, or organization.

34. (D) Ad hoc

Ad hoc is when a business encounters a problem and creates a solution to that problem spontaneously rather than having pre-planned expectations on how to handle such an occurrence.

35. (B) Alliance

An agreement in which the parties involved come together because it will benefit everyone involved is commonly known as an alliance.

36. (A) Angoff

The Angoff method is used to determine the likelihood of an average score for standardized testing as pertains to entrance exams for potential employees or employees seeking a promotion. The process works by using a set of experts to review the tests, outline the typical candidate who will be taking that test, and determine the likely score of the test on an average basis.

37. (B) Arbitration

Arbitration is a process that allows parties to take a legal matter before a judge. In doing so, the parties involved waive their right to a jury trial and most often have no recourse to appeal should they disagree with the judge's final ruling.

38. (C) Asynchronous learning

Asynchronous learning is an online learning platform utilized by many businesses as a means of connecting instructors with students from different time zones and areas of the world and allowing them to get the training they need to enhance their career development.

39. (D) Balance sheet

A balance sheet approach is a business model that is used to outline and standardize employee salaries, benefits, and other compensation. A balance sheet helps streamline these processes and ensures equality across the board in an organization.

40. (A) Behavioral interview

A behavioral employment interview is used to assess how an individual will perform in future employment endeavors.

41. (B) Biographical data

Biographical data, also known as biodata, is a collection of information on an individual's personal, educational and professional history.

42. (A) Blended learning

Blended learning means combining multiple methods of learning in order to successfully train a desired audience or demographic. Most often this means using both in-person instruction and internet-based online learning.

43. (C) Career development

Career development is when a person's career is advanced through continued education, training, and strategic career advancement.

44. (B) Career management

Career management is when individuals take responsibility for their career goals and advancements. This is done by taking advantage of training and continuing education opportunities, applying for career opportunities when they become available and moving up the career ladder through promotions.

45. (B) Caux Principles

The Caux Principles were created by an organization of international business leaders who came together to set a standard of ethical guidelines for international business dealings.

46. (C) Consolidation

Consolidation occurs when a business wants to combine or pare down resources, reduce redundancies in operations, streamline workforces and make them more efficient, eliminate unnecessary waste, and make an organization run more efficiently in general.

47. (C) Contract manufacturing

Contract manufacturing is a specific production method used by businesses in which they outsource some or all of their production needs. Most often this outsourcing is done to keep up with production needs in the event that the host company cannot keep up with the demand for a product or is experiencing a high volume of demand due to a holiday or season.

48. (D) Cost-benefits analysis

A cost-benefits analysis is designed to analyze whether a business is likely to succeed. This is calculated by determining the start-up costs and operations cost and comparing them to the likely profitability and long-term earnings of a business.

49. (A) Cost per hire

Cost per hire is a recruiting tool that helps HR determine a budget for recruiting new employees. It involves assessing the cost of advertising, recruiting fees, job referral fees, travel expenses for employment candidates, and other similar application- or job-related fees.

50. (A) Cultural coaching

Cultural coaching involves teaching employees about specific cultural differences that they may encounter while working for a business. This kind of training is especially important for companies that work internationally with others that have a vastly different cultural makeup than their own. An example of cultural coaching might be an American employee who gets cultural coaching for a new client coming from Korea.

51. (B) Days to fill

Days to fill is the term used to account for the time that it typically takes for the HR personnel in an organization to advertise a position, interview employment candidates, vet qualified candidates, complete reference checks, and hire the appropriate employee.

52. (C) Distance learning

Distance learning uses an assortment of materials to provide continued education through remote learning. This type of learning most often works best for employers who have employees in different time zones or in different countries. It allows employees to be flexible with when they do their training or learning while ensuring they still are taught the same material as everyone else. Training videos, software programs, live streams, and prerecorded videos are just a few of the ways that distance learning can be utilized.

53. (D) Retention

Document retention is an important business practice under local, state, and federal laws. There are certain documents a business must hold onto for a set period of time before those documents are destroyed. Some of those documents may include tax forms, employment forms, personal employee information, and permits.

54. (A) Employee assistance program

Employee assistance programs offer assistance to employees when it comes to resolving personal issues outside work, which may interfere with an individual's overall work performance, productivity, or attendance. These programs may include counseling services, addiction or rehab services, support for personnel with family members who suffer from substance abuse, assistance for employees who have terminal family members, among others.

55. (B) Employee handbooks or manuals

An employee handbook or manual outlines the organization's mission statement, the goals of the company, the benefits available through that organization, codes of conduct, additional compensation offered, policies and procedures, and any other pertinent information. An employee handbook often has a form that an individual must sign to confirm that he/she has received and read the document.

56. (C) Employee turnover

Employee turnover is the rate at which employees leave a business and create unfilled positions. It also refers to the amount of time that the organization has unfilled positions that sit vacant.

57. (D) Employer-paid benefits

Employer-paid benefits are provided to employees and staff at no cost to them. These benefits are in addition to a salary.

58. (B) A business' company culture

Company culture is the beliefs of a business and the behaviors that it deems appropriate by the individuals who make up that organization. Company culture is most often seen from a worldview perspective. It includes the language that a business uses, its values, the rules that it has and how it chooses to implement them, the processes and procedures that it puts in place, and how the company physically and verbally represents itself.

59. (D) Defined values

An organization's defined values refer to its beliefs. These beliefs are lasting and carry through the life of a business. Values are considered to be absolutes in terms of what is good and desirable and what is bad and unacceptable. These values help set the tone for a business' company culture.

60. (A) Vision statement

A vision statement is a declaration of what a business is, what it wants to eventually become, and how it plans to reach such a goal.

61. (B) Employee handbook

An employee handbook is a compilation of information that a new employee needs to be aware of in a business.

62. (B) A large corporation with satellite offices in England, Italy, and Germany

A large corporation with satellite offices internationally would need a fully staffed and comprehensive HR department due to the number of employees.

63. (C) Job database

An organization's job database contains information on every job in the organization. It will list each job by title, list a detailed description of the duties covered under that job, set minimum qualifications needed to fill the position, and contain any additional information that may be necessary to know the type of candidate that would be best qualified to fit that position.

64. (A) Reasonable accommodations

Replacing the standard floor-to-ceiling filing cabinet with three short filing cabinets that are waist level to accommodate Olivia's needs so she can perform her job is a reasonable accommodation under the Americans with Disabilities Act.

65. (C) Age discrimination

Eleanor meets all the criteria required for the position, and she's the best candidate for the job. However, the HR manager chooses not to hire her because of her age. This type of discrimination is illegal under the Age Discrimination in Employment Act, which protects individuals age 40 or older.

66. (A) Performance

Managing a business entails paying attention to its performance and the needs of its employees.

67. (B) Team leaders

Members of management who are above hourly employees but below department managers and supervise only small groups of employees at a time are known as team leaders. Team leaders help guide and support employees. Additionally, they take some of the workload and responsibilities off a department manager. Team leaders can have a huge impact, especially when utilized in large-scale business and in production facilities.

68. (C) Organizational development

Organizational development utilizes behavioral science to change how a business functions through the development, improvement, reinforcement, and support of processes and structures in the business.

69. (B) Americans with Disabilities Act Amendments Act

The Americans with Disabilities Act Amendments Act was revised in 2008 and implemented in January 2009 to broaden the umbrella of who can be covered by the law, what the term *disability* means, and how significant the impairment needs to be in order for an individual to qualify for protection under the law.

70. (D) Layoffs

When a business is downsizing, it is common for layoffs to occur and typical hours to be cut. Organizations that have multiple shifts may cut back to only one or two shifts instead. Employees may be given the option to cross-train for other positions or required to take on a heavier workload.

71. (C) Business management and strategies

Business management and strategies outline how businesses set up the plan of what their business is going to be, establish their short- and long-term goals, and determine how they plan to reach those goals.

72. (A) The Clayton Antitrust Act

The Clayton Antitrust Act regulates United States business practices and is designed to make antitrust laws stronger, puts a stop to mergers that are not competitive, cuts out price gouging, and eliminates other similar unethical business practices.

73. (D) The Sherman Antitrust Act

The Sherman Antitrust Act was enacted to regulate interstate commerce throughout the United States. It also outlawed monopolies and other similar business practices.

74. (A) The Social Security Act

The Social Security Act was enacted to provide for the welfare of the elderly and handicapped. It also provides for maternal and child welfare, as well as the dependents of any such persons. The provisions under this law set up the Social Security Board, raise money for the care of such individuals, define such individuals, and provide protections, benefits, and compensation.

75. (D) The Service Contract Act

The SCA ensures that contractors that do work worth more than $2500 will be eligible to receive fringe benefits.

76. (B) The Consumer Credit Protection Act

The Consumer Credit Protection Act requires financial lenders to put the terms of all lending into terms that consumers can easily understand.

77. (C) Employee relations

Employee relations covers all things that relate to the relationships, communication, and correspondence that take place between the employees of a business and the employers or owners. Ensuring good communication and practicing appropriate conflict resolution is important in maintaining healthy employee relations.

78. (C) The Federal Insurance Contributions Act

The Federal Insurance Contributions Act is the federal law that created provisions for financing Medicare and Social Security. The law mandates that employers withhold the proper amount from employees' pay to pay into Medicare and Social Security.

79. (A) Risk management

    Risk management covers all things related to health, safety, and the prevention of injuries and illness in the workplace.

80. (D) The Federal Unemployment Tax Act

    The Federal Unemployment Tax Act was put in place to permit the United States government to tax businesses and employees for the purpose of collecting taxes that will be used to fund unemployment insurance.

81. (B) The Labor Management Reporting and Disclosure Act

    The Labor Management Reporting and Disclosure Act gives rights to union members and protects the interests that the union in question is promoting. It safeguards the funds and assets that belong to the labor organization, as well as the union members that support it.

82. (C) The Longshore and Harbor Workers' Compensation Act

    The Longshore and Harbor Workers' Compensation Act was enacted to provide compensation to workers who work in United States harbors and waterways, as well as where such vessels are built or repaired, loaded or unloaded, or otherwise worked with. In the event that an employee who works such waterways or harbors is injured or disabled, this law ensures that the person receives financial compensation, medical care, and rehabilitation services.

83. (C) The Patent Act

    The Patent Act is a federal law that protects inventions and creations from having others illegally reproduce the invention, use the invention, or make money off that invention by selling it. Patent holders have the right to issue licenses giving others written legal permission to use their invention for the terms under that particular license.

84. (D) Employee and labor relations

Employee and labor relations includes employee rights, unions, employee retention, positive employee relationships, workplace behavior, and any other such employee- and employer-related behavior.

85. (A) The Portal-to-Portal Act

The Portal-to-Portal Act gives employers the right not to pay employees for time worked before or after the job. For example, construction workers will be paid for building a house but not for the time it takes to drive from the company office to the work site.

86. (B) It clearly defines what unethical behavior is under United States federal law.

The Clayton Antitrust Act was passed to specifically define unethical business practices. The law regulates business practices, places bans on anticompetitive mergers, prohibits price discrimination and unethical behavior by companies, protects consumers, and gives them the right to protest.

87. (C) The Public Contract Act

Under the Public Contract Act, any contract that is over $15,000 and takes place in the United States is protected. The Public Contract Act requires the United States government to ensure fair wages, limit working hours, and regulate health and safety standards for contracted work.

88. (A) The Railway Labor Act

The Railway Labor Act is a federal law that allows railroad and airline workers to strike for unfair working conditions in opposition to mediation or arbitration.

89. (C) To have current information on the jobs in a business and what is required to fill them if they become vacant

A job analysis gives HR a database that can be added to as needed as an organization grows. It lists what the job requires so that proper candidates can be recruited if the position becomes vacant. It also shows what the job itself entails.

90. (A) W-4 form

The W-4 form is a document that employees must fill out to indicate their tax status with the employer that is hiring them. The W-4 form indicates what the employer should be holding back in taxes from the employees' pay based on their marital status, number of dependents, and any additional allowances or other concessions the employee wishes to pay into taxes.

91. (C) Employment at will

An employment-at-will arrangement allows either the employee or the employer to end the employment contract for any reason at any time. Such a contract does not require an employer to have good cause when firing an employee, and an employee is not required to give a reason for leaving the job.

92. (C) The Consolidated Omnibus Budget Reconciliation Act

COBRA allows employees who are hit with layoffs to maintain health-care coverage for themselves and their families for a time.

93. (B) Mobile device application

In today's world, most people use a cell phone to communicate both personally and for business reasons. As a result, businesses and hiring agencies are now utilizing phone apps to attract more job candidates.

94. (B) 40 and over

The Age Discrimination in Employment Act provides protection for those who are 40 years of age or older from being discriminated against based on their age in regard to hiring, firing, or promoting.

95. (D) Outsource

Smaller businesses will often outsource part or all of their HR department duties. Outsourcing may include payroll or benefits programs.

96. (A) Hands-on learning

Teaching Hector to do his job while on the line is known as hands-on learning or on-the-job training. This is an especially good teaching method for those who best learn kinesthetically.

97. (B) Based on the amount of work they have put in and how well they have done their job

A merit raise is a raise that employees earn based on the amount of effort and work they put into their jobs. Effort, hours, work, and commitment shown are often directly reflected in the amount of a merit raise.

98. (A) Hazard pay

Employees are most often given a raise, bonus, or pay in addition to a typical salary as compensation for working in a field or location that puts their life or health in imminent danger.

99. (B) Workers' compensation

Employees who are hurt while on the job are entitled to benefits under workers' compensation laws.

100. (D) HR

The key functions of HR are to produce, develop, compensate, integrate, and maintain. HR *produces* through job analysis, recruitment, selection, placement, onboarding, transfers, and promotions. HR *develops* through performance appraisal, training, career planning, development, and transition planning. HR *compensation* is done through evaluation, wages and salary, bonuses and incentives, and payroll. HR *integrates* labor relations, motivation, grievances, and discipline. Finally, HR *maintenance* is done through health and safety, risk management, social security, welfare, and record-keeping.

References

https://www.hrci.org

https://www.pearsonvue.com/hrci

https://www.youracclaim.com/org/hr-certification-institute/badge/associate-professional-in-human-resources-aphr

Made in the USA
Monee, IL
08 July 2021

73207777R00144